Transnational Tourism

*Globalization Challenges
and Opportunities*

Dr. Denis Ushakov

ISBN: 978-0-244-11541-8

Contact the author at:
denisushakov@pnwriter.org

Contents

INSTEAD OF INTRODUCTION...

Globalization is one of the most important and decisive features in the world economic development today. It has not only changed the whole production process as such but has also institutionalized all factors, technologies and means of production, thus making it possible using the key advantages of various national economic systems within the international process of value creation. Globalization has also transformed most of fundamental macro- and microeconomic principles and norms, including those of competition, pricing, public regulation etc.

From the very beginning of globalization-related changes international tourism was among the pioneers of all new global trends. This is mostly because this type of commercial activity assumes direct interaction of factors with different national affiliations. Also, international tourism assumes the creation of common information, legal and cultural space so that to increase the quality of tourist product, taking into account individual preferences of each traveller.

One of the globalization-related consequences for international tourism is rapid emergence and development of transnational corporations in this sector. Already back in the 20th century they emerged as a radically new form of management and production process organization. And this newer form of management has allowed not only boosting the competitiveness growth but also obtaining the whole range of competitive advantages of the global scale.

TNCs in tourism have several specific features, in particular: unique organizational structure, global-scale strategies, close direct intracorporate relations and communications etc.

Research on key features of transnational corporations' functioning in the tourism sector in their interaction with other actors at the international tourism market (including national state authorities) seems to be topical and timely these days since such research would contribute to determination of the methods and instruments to be applied for the "breeding" of own, national tourist corporations which are supposed to have sufficient competitiveness level as compared to other large players at the world market of tourism. In this context, newly emerged models and patterns of interaction (including those between a foreign tourist TNC and a recipient state) would require radical liberalization of the sector and also significant shifts in national priorities and vision.

Our research rests on the assumption that transnational organization of tourist services' production under today's conditions is already the only form, truly able to provide competitive advantages of the adequate global level. Consequently, the process of world tourism consolidation is one of the core objective preconditions for the functioning of international tourist market, and adaptation to its specificity and requirements is the top-priority task for any national state directly involved in the process of international tourists' exchange.

Therefore, the aim of this monograph has been studying the key peculiarities in transnational organization of mass tourist services' production as well as full-scale scientific reconsideration of this phenomenon which would have been impossible to do from the standpoint of classical theories of the world trade.

Since the very process of tourism sector transnationalization is a multifaceted one, with several distinct stages in the course of its historic development as well as with its own consequences of economic, political, social and managerial nature, analysis of this process would require a complex approach to solving several following tasks:

- to determine the key historic stages in transnationalization of tourist activities along with the evolutionary forms of TNCs operating in tourism. This can be done after analyzing the dynamics of the external environment factors' development along with the key features in organization of transnational tourist services' production (and these features would be different for each of development stages);

- to analyze the key features of today's tourist transnational corporations along with the potential directions in their future development;

- to explain the economic efficiency of contemporary transnational tourism business and also to define the sources of global competitiveness for TNCs operating in the tourism sector along with the ways how to exploit these sources in the course of tourist services' production;

- to detect what are the most topical problems with efficiency of tourist services' production at the transnational level along with the key problems related to interaction of TNCs with the recipient states. The role of TNCs as the carriers of technological progress in the world tourism is explained, and TNCs are also presented as the initiators of global universalization in products and services;

- to describe the types of transnational corporations in tourism from the standpoint of the existing approaches to typology of corporate models (American, European and Muslim); to outline advantages, bottlenecks and prospects for each of them;

- to study the contemporary approaches to the process of organizational structure formation by a TNC. On the basis of best practices' analysis on the examples from transnational tourism and hospitality business, to present the key directions in transformation of organizational structures within the well-consolidated tourism sector, taking into account, on the one hand, the key advantages of TNCS, and on the other - general conditions of global competition.

The research object in this monograph is international tourism as a multifactor socioeconomic phenomenon which is in cause-effect relations with the world economy in general, both being also under

3

the influence of globalization, transnationalization and liberalization processes.

The research focus is on determining transnational activities at the global tourism market as an essentially new type of production organization in the field of tourist services. And this new type of services' production is grounded and explained in detail.

Chapter 1

HISTORICAL FORMS OF TOURISM GRADUAL TRANSNATIONALIZATION AND THE PERPETUUM MOBILE BEHIND IT

ABSTRACT

For the last 70 years tourism has been always at the forefront of business transnationalization, since it has been consistently exploiting all advantages of transnational production & distribution system, thus forming additional competitive advantages of the truly global scale.

The first chapter below defines transnationalization as a contemporary form of tourism and hotel business organization. It was introduced directly by entrepreneurs as one of the potential solutions to classical market problems (including limitedness of demand and production factors).

These market problems became especially severe in the second half of the previous century and all of them directly influenced tourism development.

The chapter analyzes the driving forces behind transnationalization of tourism and hospitality sectors, taking into account the economic effect from transnationalization synergy.

Transnationalization: Unconventional Solutions For Typical Problems Of The Market

Transnational corporations today are the major organizational engine of the world economy. Intracorporate labor distribution today decides for the traditional labor distribution inside many countries worldwide, not the opposite. For all these corporate organizational structures international economic relations form the external environment. Acting in accordance with the key aim (which is profit maximization, just as in any other business) transnational corporations are constantly on the move, they are always in the process of modification which concerns both their strategy and structure. And this constant process of change has today the most significant impact on the formation of international economic relations.

Today's corporations cover about two thirds of the world trade *(Data https://www.investopedia.com/terms/m/multinationalcorporation.asp)*. They are also the key player in development and distribution of the most advanced technologies. Corporations, at the same time, have enormous demand for additional capital inflow and huge cash surplus. Therefore, they are doomed to become also the key players at all world financial markets. Apart from purely economic role, many corporations have a cultural one too: through distribution of their products worldwide corporations also export cultures. However, we are convinced that the most significant impact from multinational corporations falls on the service sector: internationalization of services today has the widest geographical coverage.

As it was well described in (Wilkins, 1992), multinational company does not simply relocate from one country to another. It goes far beyond the borders of its motherland. It remains to be present in a country of headquarters, however, it is also present in an enormous number of other countries. Its package which includes management and organizational capacities does not know political borders as such. Multinational company is thus founding (or buying, in some cases) and then managing a network of interrelated enterprises *(Wilkins, 1992)*.

As it is with many other complex notions, there is no common, international acknowledged and universally approved definition of what is transnational corporation.

In the widest sense, transnational corporation means a company producing commodities and/or providing services in more than one country. In a narrower sense, this is an enterprise which uses direct foreign investments (FDI) to manage and control all its branches in several countries, apart from the country of its headquarters *(Borrus et al., 1997)*. In this case, FDI volumes are turning into the key indicator of the international production development. However, this, in turn, leads to underestimation of production transnationalization since FDI make up only about a quarter of all investments into international production, while the systems of global production and distribution are becoming less and less dependent upon ownership and/or management factors, and today look more like many very separate companies united in networks for transborder production.

Any attempt to provide a universal, acceptable for all definition of a transnational corporation is doomed to fail since the organizational structure of international corporations is very dynamic and it is changing as quickly as international economic relations are changing. A relatively compromised variant of a definition has been suggested by the UN Center on Transnational Corporations *(Borrus et al., 1997)*:

- TNC is a company consisting of two or more units, regardless their legal form of ownership and/or field of activity;

- its decision-making allows carrying out a well-coordinated policy and have one common strategy as well as one managing center;

- it is a company in which separate business units are connected with each other by means of property or in some other way so that one or more of them have profound influence on the others.

7

This influence, inter alia, concerns the distribution of knowledge, resources and responsibilities.

Therefore, we can state that the basis of TNC definition is the number of countries involved in business operations – at least two (though some definitions state three, not two). However, even such a simplified approach is extremely formal. From the standpoint of a real company, problems arise already at the stage of doing business in two countries – there appear new business risks, and there are also differences in cultural communication etc. The more countries a company has within its business environment – the more complex these problems become, however, the contents of these problems does not change essentially.

Determining the key features of some abstract transnational corporations does not seem to be possible either, actually. As of today, any large business is international by default. This is happening due to growing liberalization of international relations and openness of markets. Under such conditions maintaining one strong competitive advantage of a business in one country only would be still possible only provided it is using full set of advantages from international labor distribution.

Below we would like to outline several key features of transnational corporations which make them different from other enterprises operating at external markets *(Ushakov & Simasathiansophon, 2016)*:

- detachment from any national ground, truly global character of corporate planning. All operations on supply and distributions are centralized under private control;

- international distribution of labor is applied within a complex system of technologically interrelated enterprises in several countries which are exchanging unfinished goods applying not commercial, but transfer pricing;

- all markets are divided between corporate branches, however, their technological support remains to be centralized.

8

The reasons behind emergence and development of transnational companies can be versatile, however, all of them are, to some extent, related to market imperfection and all the limitations existing on the way of world trade development. Other strong reasons also include unfair monopolies, currency exchange control by the states, differences in tax regimes between the countries and serious transport expenses *(Movsesyan, 2001)*.

International Tourist Market On Its Way To Transnationalization

Thorough research of the international travels' market evolution allows defining a range of historic stages in the course of its development which this market has passed on its way to establishing strong international connections and interaction.

Initially (till the middle of the previous century) international tourism resembled world trade in its very classical form. All national tourist operators were functioning in the context of standard trade relations with foreign suppliers (hotels, transport companies, public catering facilities etc.). At the same time, these tourist operators were forming tourism products which clearly had national features and were strongly affiliated to a particular tourist service. Low volumes of international tourist exchange as well as transport underdevelopment, imperfect communication means were hindering the development of tourism worldwide, thus making the economy of scale an impossible phenomenon for tourism business.

Intensive development of technologies, more availability of air transport and communications becoming much cheaper (especially, emergence and quick development of e-communications) – all contributed significantly to radical socioeconomic changes in the last quarter of the 20th century. These changes included welfare level rise, more leisure time for all employees, more convenient pensions, reduced number of families with more than two children, increased share of female employment etc. All these factors, to various extent, contributed to popularization of international travels and the growth of tourism flows in Western countries. Due to quick scale effect and low entry barriers at many markets the tourism business worldwide experienced an impressive growth which, in its turn, led to escalation of competition at all popular tourism markets. Price competition became most important among all types of competition, since now representatives of the middle class formed the largest share of tourist operators' clients, and this group of consumer was, and still is, very worried about the spending issue.

The attempts to minimize the prime cost of tours have shown tour operators that reduction of transaction costs would be a must. Other "musts" included the guaranteed quality of tourist services at foreign resorts and relative free from competitors field for further activities. These necessities have logically led to the inflow of direct investments into foreign tourism industries in other countries of the world. Increased investment activity in the field of international tourism was also provoked by the increased concentration of capital in Western economies mostly. Other accompanying reasons included the growing profitability of tourism businesses (overall, much higher than the same indicator of many industries and especially when compared to agriculture) as well as very promising prospects for further activities (these prospects were mostly stemming from the fact that many economically weak countries had unique tourism resources).

The growth of foreign investments symbolized the beginning of the second stage in the course of tourism market globalization, the so-called internationalization which meant, first of all, the spread of stable tourist connections. These connections were mostly one-way, as between a country-donor and a country-recipient. Another key feature of this stage in the international tourism development is more close interaction of tourism production processes in two (or more) countries. This closer interaction meant that any tourism service, being part of tourism product, was gradually losing its national affiliation which became first blurry, then simply invisible.

More obvious international distribution of labor in parallel to ongoing internationalization of capital have led to more intensive international economic integration, which is – putting it in simple terms – national economies getting closer and adjusting to each other. Other contributing factors to these processes were increased mobility of labor force and gradual opening of many national economies to the world.

International tourism as a complex integrated economic system unites all processes of tourism production in one process covering many countries. However, this process must be supported by the corresponding set of political and economic priorities of public authorities in the countries promoting international tourism development (this includes, first of all, elimination of barriers to capital and labor force relocation and parallel formation of similar barriers in relation to third countries). Previous way of tourist services' production, which used to be according to the classical theories of the world trade, becomes impossible in the recipient country, even taking into account all its natural and acquired competitive advantages, unless there is active participation of a donor country too – through capital, labor force, technologies and a wide range of commodities related to tourism consumption.

Donor country is freely participating in tourist service production in a recipient country, often under the conditions of monopoly or oligopoly, thus guaranteeing not only growth of tourism sector capacities but also growth in quality of national tourism product as such. In parallel to that usually go the efforts of the investors from the tourism donor country. These investors are trying to promote the tour product of a particular recipient country at own market, thus deepening the international labor division and emphasizing the difference in positioning between the country "for work" and the country "for leisure" (soon popular tourism destination). This division eventually has its positive impact on investment attractiveness of tourism sector in a recipient country.

Transnationalization, therefore, has become the peak in evolution of the international tourism market, and its major preconditions were the following consequences from international economic integration:

- Growing effect of scale in tourism business when international traveling became truly large-scale;

- Spread of information technologies and communication means worldwide, formation of a single, planetary-level information field, freely available from nearly any location on the planet and accessible for the unlimited number of users simultaneously;

- Significant improvements in transportation means which are breaking many geographical limitations in the course of international tourist exchange development;

- Drastic reduction of transportation and communication costs due to advanced technologies; processing, saving and further use of information became significantly cheaper too;

- Easy access and same easy circulation of knowledge and technologies contributing to creation of new tourism products, their promotion and more intensive sales. One of the manifestation of this feature became popularity of getting a degree in Tourism Business, Hospitality etc.;

- Wider spread of international forms of production and other economic activities (frameworks of organizational forms in this case are larger than national borders and are truly international, thus contributing to the formation of one common marketplace);

- Overall liberalization of the world trade;

- Concentration of capital in a few financial centers worldwide;

- Gradual unification of accounting, statistics, taxation etc.;

- Unification of standards in the fields of services;

- Higher mobility of population on the planet overall due to weakening roles of habits, traditions, classical social connections, customs etc. People today have all the means, both external and internal, to go beyond national limits;

- Unification of consumer preferences, worldwide popularization of one-for-all "proper and up to date" lifestyle;

- Growing influence of supranational organizations, including those engaged in regulation of the world tourism flows.

Transnational tourist business can be defined as a socioeconomic phenomenon which depends today not as much on national, intrastate issues but more on external factors, the contents and the number of which is predetermined by the world community, the members of which, in their turn, are interconnected with each other in all spheres of social life, including economy, politics, ideology, cultural, environmental work, security etc.

Analysis of tourism business evolution allows determining the key preconditions required for its transnationalization. Transition to the transnational level of management looks like the only possible solution to which this business sector is being pushed by a range of imperfections in contemporary market relations. Tourism market, just as any other market today, cannot be perfect due to several reasons, the contents of which remain unchanged for over 50 years by now, even though the forms of these reasons and their manifestations may change.

Synergy In Tourist Service Production: How To Evoke And Maintain It

The synergy theory seems to be universal when it comes to scientifically grounded definition of the phenomenon "transnationalization of tourist services". The key here is strong managerial motivation of a company to shift to the transnational level of management with the aim to reach the synergy effect in the course of integration and further joint activities of a parent company and its foreign branches *(Bradley et al., 1988)*.

The key notion of this theory is synergy itself – understood here as activity of two or more subjects, in the course of which there emerges an additional effect from their interaction, apart from the direct results each side gets from this cooperation. Within the frameworks of this theory, integration and transnationalization

13

generate synergy as an added value of a new participant. This is happening due to the fact that this integrated participant uses a wider range of advantages emerging in the course of integration (through exchange of experiences, technologies, scale effect etc.).

We can outline two key directions in which synergy may emerge in the process of tourist services' transnationalization.

First of all, this is the synergy effect from the increasing economic weight of a tourism corporation which is able to guarantee wider choice in economic propositions and better conditions overall due to the emergence of new capacities, larger volumes of sales and bigger share of the consumer market. Besides that, huge transnational company gets a chance to impose certain pressure on other participants of the same market, including competitors and key partners. Moreover, it is able to use this pressure on consumers as well as on state regulatory bodies.

The second important direction for the synergy effect to reveal itself in the course of tourism business transnationalization is related to company's newly emerged capacity to use available resources more efficiently. This concerns not only financial or material resources, but also marketing ones, and also know-hows, virtual space of the company etc. The leapfrogging growth of efficiency from the corporate resources' use becomes real in the course of company's transition to the transnational level due to scale effect, centralization of certain functions, elimination of functions' doubling and also due to more efficient use of capital and information resources, use of advanced methods in operational and HR management, diversification of activities and proposition etc. *(Savchuk, 2002)*.

Therefore, the motivations behind tourism business transnationalization include, on the one hand, the increased value per each business participant involved in the process of transnationalization due to more efficient management and elimination of doubled functions. And on the other hand, this motivation includes enlargement of the participants themselves, since now they are able to save on expenses, attract more resources and thus increase their capitalization *(Rudykh, 2000)*.

14

Let us consider in more detail some of the synergy effects that may arise as a result of tourism business transnationalization. The most important synergy effect for tourism is the effect of scale which in many cases can be considered as the criterion of company's competitiveness. Scale effect is manifested as a significant decrease in prime cost of one unit of a tourist product due to growth of its sales' volumes. Scale effect has several sources of origin, and their complex use in tourist service production may only reinforce the synergy.

Any tourist corporation has its load of regular expenditures, which are not always determined by the production volumes or by other variables such as sales volumes, for example. Prime cost of a standard tour package of services is determined by a complex set of dynamically developing variables in their interconnection. The specificity of tourist service production is that variable expenses in it have much more impact than fixed ones.

For example, variable expenses of a standard tourist service production include services by independent suppliers, starting with hotel owners and ending with insurance companies, and their percentage share in a tour package may significantly vary. Fixed expenses in tourism business include rental payments, advertisement costs, salaries of own staff (those positions which have no immediate influence on the sales volumes, like accountants, planners, advertisement agents etc.). The share of fixed expenses in the prime cost of a final product even in small tourism business does not go above 15%, while the much larger share of spending falls on various payments for suppliers' services.

Moreover, added value, generating the profit for a tourist company, is created exactly in the process of tour operator's interaction with suppliers of tourism services. Tour operator functions under constant two-sided pressure: on the one hand, demand generated by the consumer market is always limited; and on the other hand, there is always pressure on the side of suppliers who are driven by the uniqueness of own services and thus are able to consider some of tour operators as second rate (depending on the list of clients they currently have). Thus, suppliers always have a chance to dictate their conditions for further cooperation, reducing the interest margin and making tour operators overall less flexible and more economically dependent.

Tourism sector, more than any other branch, is prone to such dependencies, mostly due to seasonality of tourism demand and also due to significant fluctuations at consumer markets which may happen even in the course of one season. For example, hotels in a particular location/area, observing higher than expected demand due to some external (not depending on the hotels themselves or on tour operators) causes, may send their prices soaring and thus reconsider all prior agreements with operators at the market. Such cases are not rare at this market, therefore, they tend to increase the potential risks for tour operators due to the fact that both demand and supply are highly unstable and prone to sudden changes at the tourism market.

On the other hand, suppliers in tourism are trying to avoid their own risks and thus prefer to cooperate with tourism companies under the so-called risk schemes: when the risk of a supplier (which mostly concerns idle periods at places of service production) is fully shifted on tourism companies. The latter are forced to purchase quotas (a certain number of rooms, for example) for the season, however, they are also able in this case to establish their own commission fee for further sale to tourists. Under such a risk scheme, the tour operator bears all the risks in case of an idle period (when a room is not occupied by tourists and/or when the board of a plane is half empty). These risk schemes are mostly used by rather confident in their capacities tour operators that have enough marketing and financial opportunities to guarantee a certain threshold number of tourists throughout the whole season. In case this threshold is not reached, huge volumes of spending on the suppliers would simply turn into losses from the unused rooms and/or never purchased plane tickets.

Therefore, only tour operators with large market shares and stable distribution channels dear to implement these risk schemes with their suppliers. And this is the first source of scale effect in tourism service production. Clearly, the larger is the share of a particular company, the more risks it can afford in its operations and schemes, mostly because large-scale preorders also means higher discounts from suppliers, hotels and air companies first of all.

However, the potential of these risk schemes as an instrument to get the maximum scale effect is limited by the market proposition itself and also may be limited by the commercial interests of a particular supplier. For a tour operator today the availability of certain number of preordered rooms (or even of the whole venue) is not a competitive advantage anymore, this factor has already become a must, a necessity for further survival under the conditions of ongoing price wars. Besides that, even under the risk scheme with a tour operator, suppliers remain to be rather independent in both decisions and operations, and this is always a significant threat to the strategic interests and stability of tour operators, since for the latter services provided by various suppliers within the same package are treated as some sort of investments in intangible assets.

Promotion of a hotel at regional markets is also carried out at the expense of a tour operator, while all strategic advantages from this advertisement later belong to the hotel itself. Under such conditions, when any hotel and any airline has the right to withdraw from cooperation with a tour operator (keep in mind that the latter has long-term investments of own capital, labor and efforts in the intangible assets of a supplier), the company itself would not be very much interested in these investments, if only supplier is getting the fruits. However, these investments are still necessary if tour operator plans to obtain a strategic competitive advantage. For the same reason, tour operator has only one alternative available – to merge or buy out the supplier. And this would be a transnational tourism business unit already, within the newly emerged legal frameworks of which tourist services and tourism product would be forming in parallel and mutual compliance.

Having several managed suppliers allows tour operator not only reach the maximum possible scale effect (first of all, due to intracorporate transfer pricing for the suppliers' services) but also guarantees a whole range of new competitive advantages of not related to pricing nature. Now this particular tour operator would always be the top priority choice when the recently purchased hotel (or airline company) is considering potential partnerships. Other companies would be forced to face high prices from this supplier and less comfortable conditions overall, or they can withdraw from competition as such, thus giving away their market share. Besides that, if the tour operator buys out a supplier, they guarantee themselves automatically additional stability in further implementation of their strategic interests. Therefore, later on they may allow themselves much more freedom of investing in both tangible and intangible assets of the now affiliated company, being absolutely sure there would be no unexpected changes in its further market behavior.

Therefore, vertical integration in tourism business can go in two directions: purchasing a business supplier (downward growth) or purchasing a tourist agent (upward growth). Both would eventually lead to the increased effect of scale achieved mostly due to optimization and reconsidered, not internal, pricing policies (the latter means, first of all, establishing discriminatory prices for the outside partners).

The second source of the scale effect emerging in transnational tourism business is formed by transaction costs, that is, the costs of a tourist operator, not directly related with the production activities, neither with the process of these production activities' planning and organization *(Ushakov & Simasathiansophon, 2016)*. Transaction costs in tourism are predetermined by the necessity to create and maintain in full operation the efficient communication channels connecting all participants of a production process (suppliers, tourist operator, tourist agents, corresponding public authorities, unions of consumers, other partners etc.). When this tourism production process involves mostly independent parties, transaction costs start to grow significantly due to the necessity to invest more in the creation of efficient communication channels which are vitally important for universalization of standards between these independent partners and creation of common for all stimuli to maintain efficient performance and stable communication. Moreover, multiproduct tourist operator, having a large partner database, is almost forced to create versatile, by structure and contents, communication channels for further works with its very different partners. For example, tourist operator has to take into account language peculiarities, time zones, mentality, religion and other factors. This, obviously, also increases the transaction costs.

While in the case of transnational corporation transaction costs will be reduced rather quickly and dramatically, mostly due to the introduction of common corporate standards (for example, in financial reporting) and/or common stimuli to increase the efficiency of intracorporate communication. For transnational corporation savings on transaction costs may reach hundred thousands and in some cases even millions of USD, and these savings will eventually also contribute to the scale effect from tourism production.

Finally, the third source of scale effect in transnational tourist activities is related to savings on tax payments due to specificity of planning which takes into account the peculiarities of taxation regimes in all related states and territories where its branches and other affiliated structures are located.

Using intracorporate financial flows, top management of a corporation can legally manage their income and thus declare income only in the states with most favorable taxation, and on the opposite – corporation can withdraw income from the territories with unfavorable taxation regime using the instruments of transfer pricing and internal payments. This is one of the options how strategic competitive advantages of separate states can be used in transnational activity to increase the efficiency of transnational tourism production manifold.

The second synergy effect arising due to transnationalization of tourism activities is the growth in quality of tourism product.

This growth in quality has several key components, one of which is the guarantee that all tourist services mentioned in a tour package will be provided in the needed volume. Growth of quality is often inversely correlated with the number of tourist services' suppliers within the same tour package. The more suppliers one tourist operator has involved in organization of one specific tourist product

– the more complicated it would be to control the process of services' provision, and their quality especially. Therefore, increase in quality of tourist services would be possible only under the very limited number of tourist service suppliers. This dependence became known to businessmen in the field back in the 1970s already, same applies to minimization of tour package prime cost as the primary cause for transnationalization of tourist activities.

Fully acquiring tourist suppliers or at least participating with own capital in their management, the tourist operator gets the capacity of nearly total control over the quality of all services within a tour package. Thus, the tour operator is able to impose common standards of servicing in various countries worldwide and in this way provide maximum guarantees their tourists get services in full volume and of best quality.

The third synergy effect can be obtained by transnational tourist companies at financial markets. This effect is preconditioned by the fact that these companies are usually more attractive and thus get better conditions for borrowing additional resources they need for their further corporate development. Financial markets allow them get such additional resources from various countries and territories worldwide simultaneously. These financial flows may originate from various countries and at the same time they can inflow to various affiliated branches of a corporation, also worldwide, and then, be further redistributed via intracorporate channels, in full accordance to the general strategy of the company. Therefore, transnational tourist corporation is able, on the one hand, to take full advantage of cross-country economic differences for its tourist services' production, and on the other hand, it is also able to overcome national bottlenecks which hinder its business development on a particular geographical territory (for example, the so-called "financial hunger" at the markets of developing countries).

TNCs of the tourist sector get their own unique capacity to "extract" funds from more financially saturated markets on the most comfortable for them conditions, including low interest rates on loans. They are also able to attract investors from the most developed countries of the world, with their surplus funds. Further, they are able to redistribute the attracted assets through their internal financial channels, allocating them in the branches which they find to be potentially most profitable. This synergy effect cannot be achieved by other tourist companies, those of not yet transnational level of management. Thus, the latter have to adapt their businesses to the peculiarities of economic systems in different countries, taking into account their numerous advantages and disadvantages. While TNCs in this case take some sort of supranational position and get the unique opportunity to combine competitive advantages of tourism productions in different countries but within the same production process.

Even if we do not take into account the capacity of a TNC to attract financial assets into its own business on the maximum comfortable and profitable conditions and even if we limit, for the purposes of our discussion, the field of transnational business activities to one state only, the investment attractiveness of large, vertically integrated corporation is in any case higher than that of a traditional tourist operator or even that of a group of tourist operators working under one brand. Consequently, corporation always gets more chances for large investments into own business and further stimulation of its development. Return on investment and their profitability in a TNC would be always higher due to a huge gap between itself and the closest competitors in terms of prices (which, in turn, are predetermined by the scale effect).

The fourth synergy effect of transnational companies can be achieved due to market share growth, up to the level of a monopoly at certain regional tourist markets. One of the specific features of tourism service production is that regional tourism markets (including those where TNCs operate) are much stronger interdependent than, for example, commodity markets. Therefore, achieving monopoly at a certain market, even if this particular market is not that important in terms of business development, would in any case strongly improve company's position and rank at other regional markets. For example, if a German corporation, being ranked third or fifth at German tourism market, achieve monopoly position in, say, Tunisia or Malaysia – this will provoke further restructuring of German tourism market, since preferences of German tourists will change in favor of these destinations rather quickly. Consequently, stimulation of German tourist demand for Tunisia or Malaysia destinations would strengthen significantly the national ranking of the corporation with monopolistic position at other markets.

This correlation explains the expansionary policies of European and American tourist corporations which are trying to find new perspective destinations for further development of European and American outbound tourism. For example, US companies are heavily investing these days in Mexican tourism sector as well as in other destinations within the Caribbean, while Europeans are concentrating their attention and investments on the North of Africa and also on the Middle East. In their attempts to monopolize the proposition at these and other markets, the TNCs are thus trying to reach monopoly at consumer markets *(Andreeva at al, 2016)*.

Monopolization of regional tourism markets provides a wide range of advantages for TNCs, including better maintained relations with local suppliers (M&As in this case become senseless due to monopolistic position of a corporation in a region in any case), trade unions and public authorities responsible for tourism development in a region. In this case corporations use these advantages not only for own development and intensified production of services, but also to maintain its monopolistic position at a market for as long as possible, often using for this artificial entry barriers. Additionally, if corporation has the capacity to impose, indirectly, the administrative pressure on its competitors – this chance will be surely used.

The fifth synergy effect from tourism business transnationalization concerns the centralization of one common system for the production processes' management. Centralization of a TNC means none of the functions is doubled, it also means there is absolute compliance between the objectives of various departments and branches. Both these features of centralization also mean that the current spending of a corporation will go down. Besides that, centralization also means universalization of rules and standards in all spheres, starting from financial reporting and ending with direct servicing of tourists. Such universalization makes corporation's position at the international tourism market only stronger, since it increases the efficiency of all marketing tools applied and contributes to consumer loyalty which is always vital under the conditions of severe competition.

The sixth synergy effect from transnationalization of tourism business concerns corporation's capacity to accumulate necessary means and information for further innovative growth. Significant financial capacities of transnational corporations and also their presence in various regions worldwide at the same time contribute greatly to accumulation of corporate managerial experience through consolidation of knowledge and organizational skills for more efficient production of tourism services. This consolidation of knowledge and skills also contributes to formation of corporate reserves for further self-development and self-education within corporation itself. This means that corporation is able to not only introduce the latest innovation in its practical activities but also to develop its own new technologies, especially when it comes to business processes' organization, promotion, marketing, HR management etc. Moreover, such self-learning corporation is able to not only develop innovative organizational technologies but later also implement them at the international tourism market. Obviously, traditional, smaller enterprises also operating within the tourism sector do not have sufficient financial resources (or access to them) so that to develop and use such innovations. A classical tourism-sector enterprise is always in need of certain volume of circulating capital. Thus, even provided it has enough information/knowledge/creativity/skills to invent a technology, it would never be able to implement it independently in its daily practical activities due to financial limitations.

The seventh synergy effect is closely related to the third and the sixth ones at the same time. It concerns the capacity of transnational tourism corporations to have immediate direct access to the resources involved in tourism services' production, including capital and technologies first of all and tourist resources too (that is, objects of tourists' interest) as well as qualified enough personnel, directly involved in servicing of tourists and in organization of transnational production of tourism services overall.

Finally, we need to mention such synergy effect from transnational tourism business as diversification of proposition. Transnational business has rather high safety margin, especially financial and marketing ones, and this margin allows sectoral TNCs introduce not only new tourist destination but also open up new types of activities, directly or indirectly connected with tourism.

This financial "safety cushion" enables corporations "extract funds" from circulation easily or borrow freely at financial markets worldwide, having the most comfortable for them conditions in their launch of new, often quite risky projects. At the same time, corporations have at their disposal such an important intangible asset as trademark/brand, and the latter becomes an additional factor to reduce risks of innovative activities and shorten the payback period of these new projects at the same time. This is why transnational corporations are forced to diversify their propositions much more often, and at the same time this diversification means less spending and less risks for them, as compared to traditional, smaller enterprises. Relative financial stability of TNCs means any innovation suggested by such corporation has by default longer "probation period" during which income already obtained from this innovation is already reinvested into newer productions, thus providing more and more incentives for further growth.

TO SUM UP

under transnationalization of tourism business here we imply:

- New phenomena along with qualitative changes in the course of tourist services' production, including the growth of number and general activeness of tourist TNCs, all closely connected with financial and banking sectors;

- A new stage in the process of tourist activities' internationalization, quite different from all previous stages.

This newer stage is different due to new manner of countries' and enterprises' attraction into international labor distribution, taking into account the fact that the world tourism market today is dictating new standards of quality along with some other economic indicators, for both headquarter companies and all their branches worldwide;

- A new form of tourism internationalization manifestation. This results in further development of international production within one tourist TNC, covering the production at both headquarters and all branches. Noteworthy here, corporations tend to develop first of all those services which are participating in international intrafirm cooperation;

- A new, higher level of internationalization for both production and capital, with gradual transition to the higher level of quality too;

- Expansion of tourist activities of the sectoral TNCs along with their gradual transformation into influential subject of the world economy.

All of the considered above synergy effects from tourist business transnationalization have nearly simultaneous impact on the process of tourist services' production. These effects are quite capable to relocate corporation to a new, higher level of management, and when this happens – products of this corporation get brand new attributes, which are necessary to achieve truly global competitive advantages.

At the same time, we should not disregard the potential negative impact from synergy in the course of tourism business transnationalization. These negative effects may be caused by the wrong assessment of merged businesses, excessive spending on expansion strategies, loss of control over the headquarters due to radical changes in management after M&A, too high turnover rate among personnel etc.

Chapter 2

BRIEF GEOGRAPHICAL AND HISTORIC OVERVIEW OF TOURISM TRANSNATIONALIZATION

ABSTRACT

The process of transnationalization in the tourism sector has a range of quite specific historical and geographical peculiarities, most of which are related to the initial stage, when local tourism business is being connected to the world processes of transnationalization and at the same time is still connected to the indicators of local tourism sector development, specificity of local tourism consumption etc. Multimodality of the world tourism development stimulates rather asynchronous dynamics of transnationalization in the regions worldwide. It has also contributed to the formation of rather complex system in global production of tourism services. Therefore, studying the peculiarities of transnationalization processes in various countries of the world during different historical periods becomes the central object for the second chapter of this monograph.

World Geography And Business Motivation Of Transnationalization Waves In Tourism And Hospitality Sectors

Transnationalization of tourism business started in the 1960s, that is, with nearly 50-year delay from the similar processes in industrial production and agriculture. The causes for this delayed inclusion of world tourism in transnationalization processes are quite obvious: the tourism sector as such started to form in the late 19th century, and only after two world wars it finally became attractive and profitable as a separate type of commercial activity and business. Thus, only much later after that its growing volumes became motivational enough to move enterprises to the transnational level of management.

Tourism as business got the distinctive feature of mass scale years after the World War II, since only then welfare of the Europeans got to the sufficient level, while family relations were transformed in a convenient for its development way (families now had less children, while the share of working women was constantly growing). An additional significant factor in tourism development was the growing social protection in many countries: more people got access to vacation leaves, pension and more stable working hours overall. Another technology-related factor in tourism development was wider spread of information and awareness: the role of various media sources – paper, radio, and later also TV and Internet – was constantly growing, thus, more and more citizens were able to get information on faraway countries for their future tourist trips.

Rapid development of communication technologies and transportation means later also contributed to diversification of tourist proposition, since even the most distanced countries and regions became "closer", traveling to various countries worldwide was getting only cheaper. Two major reasons why tourist product in general became much cheaper were: 1) scale effect; 2) significant decrease of an average tour duration, since quicker transportation meant that tourists could be delivered to the destination point faster. Another reason of prices' fall in the transportation sector was rather intensive growth of competition in this sector and emergence of newer forms of cooperation between transportation companies and tourist offices (the first charter flight, from London to Corsica, was organized back in 1950).

As it was already noted earlier, the central precondition for transnationalization of any type of production activity is growing demand as compared to decreasing entry barriers at markets. European tourist market got both these features in the middle of the previous century, when the leading – in terms of transnationalization – markets, such as agriculture, automobile construction and manufacturing, chemical products, at that time were already fully enjoying all the benefits from scale effect of production and excessive demand.

Yet another reason why tourism sector was belated in terms of transnationalization processes by at least fifty years was its low investment attractiveness and its resource base's inability to diversify. Let us compare with other industries. For example, automobile companies, on their way to transnationalization, were buying foreign industrial enterprises or even whole mining locations (for better resources' availability). Agricultural concerns, in their turn, were buying mostly land or cattle farms etc. These foreign acquisitions were quickly turning into valuable assets, the cost of which was only growing with every new year, while production capacities were expanding, being not limited to specialization and sectoral belonging of a parent company.

For example, an automobile corporation which has its own steel plant on foreign territories, in case of problems on the automobile market would be able to redesign production and use its steel in other types of manufacturing. Finally, it can simply sell the plant in case the market of industrial real estate is on its rise. In a very similar manner any transnational corporation is able to manage its foreign lands and agricultural farms.

This rather relaxed management is hardly possible in tourism business. Here logically arise the questions: what forms the foreign material & technical basis in tourism business? In what facilities abroad would transnational tourism business be interested to invest? Today the most common objects for international investments in tourism are tourist brands and associations of tourist agencies. Back in the middle of the 20th century even the most economically developed countries with a lot of interested investors hardly had any strong tourist brand or even a big tourist company with more or less stable client base, while for developing economies the very phenomenon of tourism was still rather unusual. Thus, tourist companies of the mid 20th century were mostly investing in hotels and transport companies, which were the logical and nearly the only option for them.

Transport companies of those days were often stronger (economically and in terms of marketing too) than majority of tourist firms. The former were concentrating their efforts on transportation of passengers and cargo delivery and thus had the minimum dependence upon tourist enterprises.

Moreover, buying a hotel often meant certain limitation of activities for a new owner and thus narrower specialization, since a hotel enterprise, due to specificity of its material base, is hard to redesign or restructure. Of course, a hotel can be rebuilt into an office center or into a standard residential unit, however, only in case it is situated in a convenient location (in downtown or near important crossroads etc.). Resort hotels or hotels located near highways have very little chances for successful redesigning of activities. This is especially the case with rural resort areas, with their low numbers of local population and absence of industrial production. At the same time, hotel business always has rather high level of investment risks, especially when it comes to resort areas due to very limited opportunities for diversification and dangerously tight correlation between the efficiency of local assets' use and regional development in a certain area overall.

For all of these reasons, transnationalization processes in tourism sector overall and hospitality sector especially were always lagging behind similar processes in other economic sectors. Any tourist company, willing to move forward to the transnational level in its development and management, must be aware of high entry costs (including large investment volumes so that to purchase objects abroad, their modernization and upgrade so that to comply with the world standards of servicing). Moreover, significant spending would be needed not only for purchases and upgrade but also for further promotion campaigns at own, national tourist markets so that to guarantee itself the sufficient volumes of sales. On the other hand, a tourist company, already involved in transnationalization, bears the local risks quite intentionally and is able to develop alternative scenarios of sales (for example, a local hotel in some cases can rent out its spaces to local businesses, if the volume of tourists is not sufficient enough).

The latter partially explains why foreign investors prefer, in most cases, urban hotels first of all and are less interested in resorts or highways motels (the latter become an interesting option for international investors once tourist sector in a country is developed enough to guarantee high volumes of national and international tourists' circulation). Even a very tenuous analysis of foreign investments in hospitality industries worldwide clearly demonstrates that the initial interest of investors entering countries always concerns downtowns (in the capital city first of all).

Even though such entry is always very expensive for investors (real estate in a capital city is always much more expensive than real estate on a resort line), the overall level of foreign investment risk is significantly lower. First of all, the room occupancy rate in a capital city (or other big cities) is not subject to seasonality since such hotels are mostly business-oriented, thus hospitality sector in big cities is more dependent on the state of business development overall, rather on the rate of local tourism development. Secondly, in case of a business failure, any hotel downtown can easily become an office center or can be redesigned to become a fashionable housing unit, thus selling/renting out luxury apartments instead of rooms.

Only after successful implementation of real estate project in a capital city or other large cities of a country foreign investors start considering the option of entering the real estate markets on the resort lines in the same country.

Taking into account rather narrow specialization of resort hotels, their limited opportunities to switch business and also instability of tourist demand (for example, in case of income level fall or changing tourist preferences etc.), it would be logical to assume transnational level of hospitality business can be economically feasible and profitable only in case TNC buys out not one hotel, but several hotels in different locations. This obviously means creation of a corporate hotel chain inside the TNC.

Hotel chain is a joint business which is carried out and managed using common standards of servicing and under the same trademark. In most cases hotel chain is much more efficient in its management than separate hotel businesses, again, predominantly due to scale effect. Merging several hotels into a chain allows cutting the spending manifold, especially in terms of advertising and promotion, HR preparation and management, own standards' development and unique technologies' use. Hotel chains are also much more attractive from the investors' standpoint since chains are able to offer more tempting and more efficient schemes of cooperation for both investors themselves and their wide client base too.

Establishment of an own hotel chain always requires high volumes of expenditures on the side of a founding corporation, while efficiency of local assets' use still depends more on the state of regional tourism development rather than on the capacities of a particular TNC. For this very reason, foreign investments come into hotel business only at a certain point of international tourism development in a country, once tourists' inflows become more or less stable and predictable.

First transnational deals in hotel business, interestingly, were not between a developed country and a developing one (as it was often the case in transnational agricultural business, for example) but between two developed economies. This was because international tourism of the previous century was developing primarily between already mature economies, often geographically close to each other. There were quite many reasons for this trend: transportation and communications were not developed enough yet, people still feared cultural differences and overall, the world was developing under the conditions of geopolitical bipolarity which did not contribute to tourism development at all.

European countries which were the initiators and the pioneers of integration processes in tourism, themselves fitted all necessary criteria: they were geographically close to each other, their rates of economic development were rather similar, and they were functioning under conditions of trade liberalization and cultural homogeneity. Thus, intra-European tourism provoked the emergence of European transnational companies in the sectors of tourism and hospitality.

Another stimulus for hotel businesses' transnationalization was quick popularization and spread of franchising schemes. With the emergence of franchising, entry barriers for already large European hotel chains became nearly ground level when it came to other regions worldwide. Franchising means that there is no need for own significant investments. Moreover, risks of project failure are fully on the shoulders of a local franchisee, the owner of a local hotel. At the same time, franchising brings stable incomes for a hotel chain overall and strengthens its brand both regionally and worldwide.

In the majority of cases we can observe a certain regularity: hotel chains, airline companies and large tourist enterprises from the countries which are traditional tourist donors (such as the UK, Germany, Nordic countries and also Belgium, Holland and France) were investing directly and heavily into hotel businesses located in popular destinations of European tourism – Italy, Spain, South of France, Greece and the like.

Within the tourism sector in its wider meaning, the leaders in transnationalization were hotels and airlines. First European airlines were quite strictly following the theory of related diversification, they were investing in other types of tourism activities (agent sales of air tickets, cargo deliveries and later – in networks of direct sales of tourist services). Thus, they were also interested to invest in European chains of hotels (such chains were first quite active being built near big airports and later – also at popular European resorts).

Progress in transportation and telecommunications expanded the borders of international tourist development, since it turned dozens of geographically faraway countries into popular destination points for European and American tourists. Starting from the mid-1960s European tourism market has been experiencing active interference from the side of the US hotel chains (on the territories of the United States themselves such chains were actively developing as early as the last two decades of the 19th century, thus, by the 1960s in the USA this market segment was already quite saturated). The key American feature of hotel chains' development is standardization of servicing quality, absence of specific target audience and same pricing at all venues. These trends were quickly adopted by their

European young competitors. The key differences of American hotel chains from the European model of hotel business were larger size of American hotels and their orientation on maximum presence in all the regions of expansion.

In parallel to American hotels' expansion in Europe (which also meant much larger number of American tourists coming to Europe, actually), European tourism market started to experience also the expansion on the side of airlines, banks, insurance companies etc. European hotel chains were also trying to expand in the opposite direction, however, their success on the other side of the Atlantic Ocean was much more modest: only several European hotel networks managed to open their hotels on the East Coast, in such large cities as New York, Boston, Philadelphia and New Orleans.

On the other hand, European hotels and other tourist businesses started to expand more actively in the direction of developing countries, mostly because vacations in these countries became more accessible during the 1980s. Therefore, European hotels started to be present in many locations around the Middle East, North Africa, and later also in South-East Asia and Eastern Europe, gradually reaching post-Soviet countries too. On this direction of geographical expansion, American hotels were usually the ones to follow European chains.

Tour operating and agent sectors of tourism businesses became subject to active transnationalization only in the middle of the 1980s. During the same period of time transport and communications became developed enough and services became internationalized enough so that to turn international tourism into a truly global phenomenon of massive nature. By incomes and profits, international tourism has finally outstripped automobile sector, textiles and even oil & gas. Tour operators thus became quite attractive objects for international investments. In many cases tour operators were merged with financial institutions to form holders and thus getting better access to financial resources of developed economies. At regional tourist markets stronger were becoming the largest brands, while franchising schemes were getting more and more popular, especially in the context of agents' and tour operators' work. Clients became more loyal to a particular grand, and this was actually the major reward from transnationalization of tourist business.

Early 1990s witnessed the unification of strategic management over hotel chains, airlines, tour operators and agent networks. Thus, a new network structure of tourist TNCs was gradually formed. This newer structure was already able to manage much more efficiently multiple popular brands within the common tourist market with its truly enormous material & technical base. Moreover, many tourist TNCs switched from the strategy of related diversification to the strategy of non-related diversification: they started to intrude and invest quite actively into ship-building, agriculture, aviation, high-tech sectors, retail trade, media and cinema businesses etc.

On the background of the ongoing internal restructuring of large tourist businesses which was taking place mostly through mergers and acquisitions, corporations were almost forced to impose their presence throughout the world and all economic sectors, thus expanding their network structures on newer and newer tourist destinations and other spheres of doing business.

Traditionally, the strongest positions in terms of M&As belong to the tourist transnational corporations of the USA and the EU. Japan, despite its quite impressive economic growth overall, is not on the list due to this country's very late inclusion into the world tourist production processes.

Due to geographical remoteness and specificity of Japanese mentality and lifestyle, this nation began to travel with tourist purposes relatively recently. At the same time, Japan itself, as a tourist destination, is not that popular, as compared to many other destinations in Asia, due to expensive prices and also because tourist infrastructure in this country is not that developed and adopted for international visitors. More active outbound tourism from Japan attracted more attention to the internal tourist market of this country, especially among American and European tourism-related corporations. Their quick expansion onto Japanese market was another factor contributing to slow formation and development of Japanese tourist TNCs.

Intensive processes of mergers and acquisitions at the world tourist market today confirms that contemporary tourism sector, despite its 50-year delay in transnationalization participation, has already caught up with most of industrial and technological sectors by all vital economic indicators. Therefore, world tourism today is no less attractive for large investors and international investment projects.

Previous Generations Of Tourist TNCs: Their CVs And Obituaries

Outlining comprehensively the full history of tourism business transnationalization we can determine the key historic stages in tourist TNCs' development, or their generations. These generations differ between each other by several significant features, such as the key production activity, the sources of financing, directions in the course of integration, the structure of the sector and its role at world markets.

Activities of the first generation of tourist TNCs was primarily related to transnationalization of the hotel businesses and the emergence of first international chains of hotels. This was followed by transnationalization of transportation which started in the subsectors of railway and air transport. In some cases both hotel and transport businesses managed to move to the transnational level of management rather independently, without any financial inflows from outside, that is, from more developed types of activities (Hilton hotels' chain is a good example in this regard). In other cases, both hotels and airlines reached transnational level only within vertically integrated business structures. In this case, both hotels and international transport companies were additional, non-core type of activity, e.g., for large banks, automobile holdings, retail networks etc.

Historically speaking, the first generation of tourist TNCs covered the period between 1950s and 1970s. The key features of this period were small share of international tourist exchanges and insufficient economic liberalization on the global scale. First tourist TNCs had rather limited geographical presence, and the zones of this presence were quite strictly either European, or American (the latter included both US and Canada). Geographical expansion on the markets of third countries was rather limited since international tourists flows during those days were concentrated on a few popular destinations only, and international tourism overall was hardly ever intercontinental. Besides, tourism development in third countries was an enormously expensive business since many countries had barely any tourist infrastructure (hotels, roads, transport schedule etc.). Moreover, international (and especially intercontinental) tourism was often hindered by enormous differences between the nations – cultural, economic, social, religious etc.

At the regional markets of Europe and North American first hotel chains and international transport companies were struggling in quite severe competitive fight, often trying to use the transnationaization factor to increase their overall sales' volume and thus reach monopoly. The choice of a direction for further expansion was predetermined not as much by the volume of expected costs (which was nearly always the case with first TNCs in agriculture or industrial production) but by the potential opportunities to sell services, and the latter was often dependent on tourism idea development and popularity and also on population mobility in general.

Hotel chains of the first generation were forced to overcome quite high entry barriers in new countries of their expansion due to the necessity, first of all, to build brand new hotel enterprises on literary empty grounds, moreover, they had to provide all necessary infrastructure for themselves. Since this first-generation transnationalization was so expensive, hotel chains soon became the frequent clients of all possible financial structures, since they were forced to initiate new investment projects one after another. For the same reasons, those hotel chains which were belonging to automobile concerns or retails networks, found themselves in a much more convenient and easy situation since their "parents" (for example, as in the cases of "Le Meridien" or "Sheraton") were establishing own hotel chains to reach synergy effect due to the fact that both core business and auxiliary one often had a lot of same clients (thus, their client platform became only stronger). Additional synergy was reached in these cases also due to common methods of management, similar technologies in use etc. Many industrial and especially trade corporations today are stating that during those time they somehow managed to anticipate the future tourism boom, thus, they foresaw how tourist business development could strengthen their overall stability. This was especially the case for retail trade companies since both trade and tourist services belong to the same servicing sector, thus, synergy from merging activities is higher.

However, within this first-generation TNCs tour operating business and tourist agency were present only as a minor, additional component, aimed to take care of clients visiting hotels or using the services of an inside transport company. For example, many hotel chains of those times were offering their own booking services, which covered not only hotels inside the same chain but also transport tickets. Airlines were offering additionally their rooms in certain hotels (mostly inside or nearby the largest airports of Europe and the US). Since in the middle of the 20th century mass tourism was yet to emerge – there were no all-inclusive tours, or the so-called packages. Moreover, destinations for this mass tourism appeared on the geographical map of the world much later.

The key feature of the tourist corporations of the second type is much stronger role of tour operating and tour agents. The "glory hour" of operators and agents started in the early 1970s (and lasted actually not an hour, but 15-20 years) *(Ushakov et al, 2017a)*. The key precondition for the emergence and quick development of these second-generation tourism TNCs was rapid development of mass tourism as well as expansion of geographical borders in tourism. Due to significant improvements in transportation means (especially in the subsector of aircraft) as well as progress in communications, many once exotic destinations have become easily accessible for a mass tourist. First of all, these were the countries of the Middle East and Northern Africa (for the Europeans) and also the Caribbean area and South-East Asia (for tourists from the US and Canada). The tourist product from the third-world countries was much cheaper than European or American one. Also, getting to such a faraway destination point became much cheaper since aviation was developing quite intensively in terms of technologies' used and in parallel to this technological competition was also developing quite successfully, thus contributing to prices' gradual fall. All these factors provoked truly colossal growth of tourist demand for these destinations in developed countries.

Still, these newer destinations had their problems: information on vacationing and conditions in these countries was very limited and not always trustworthy; tourists demanded certain guarantees for services' provision in full and their quality level etc. Therefore, these newer market had a truly urgent demand for tour operating and tourist agents' intrusion. Tourist firms working with these new destinations began to emerge in nearly all regions of Europe and America. With fairly equal rate they were accumulating both experience in organization of such trips and financial funds from these trips. Stable market demand stimulates wider spread of risky schemes in relations between tour operators and suppliers of tourist services (this is especially relevant in relations with airlines and hotel chains). In the middle of the 1980s tour operators and tourist agents were already not some sort of invisible intermediaries but the most valuable clients for many suppliers of tourist services. Active sales in the segments of tour operators and agents soon became an indirect but still very trustworthy guarantee for the financial wellbeing of transnational hotel and transport companies. Changed conditions require from all tourist TNCs to have own and recognizable enough brand as well as well-developed agent network. Development of both requires quite significant investments which go even higher than investments in hotel and transport networks' development.

This trend has been also stimulated by active distribution of franchising schemes in hotel business. Third countries – especially Turkey, Cyprus, Tunisia, Thailand, some of the Caribbean – have invested quite heavily (though via their private investors mostly) in the development of tourist infrastructure, construction of hotels, also building roads and providing all sorts of leisure for future tourists – from catering to entertainment. For many developing countries these were the times when international tourism became an economic priority of the state level. Expansion of hotel chains at the markets of third countries was not restrained anymore by the necessity to invest heavily, again, thanks to franchising schemes: it was enough to find an eager franchisee among the newly built hotels and make sure their internal standards comply with corporate standards of tourists' servicing.

From those time and on a geographical difference has been forming between hotel chain brand popularity worldwide and the presence of owned hotels in a particular country. Already in 1985 the number of the hotels which were nominal members of a certain hotel chain on the franchising conditions was 6,7 times higher than the number of the hotels in fact owned by the same hotel chain. Franchising also contributed to further globalization of large hotel chains: today you can book choosing between nearly identical set of hotels in all countries of the world where European and American tourists are travelling. Typical for the first generation of tourist TNCs conditions of expansion which assumed buying a hotel directly or building it from the ground level became not typical anymore: starting from late 1970s already this scheme was used only in relation to the poorest countries of the world which did not have enough own funds to construct these hotels and comply to a certain level and standards of quality.

Therefore, hotel chains were now freed from previously mandatory investments into the hotel industry. Freed financial funds became to be spent to increase the performance efficiency of tour operating companies and agent networks, both being managed by hotel chains and transport TNCs. These processes have their internal logic, at least from the standpoint of consumer demand and market nature of enterprises' functioning. Tourist TNCs started developing in the direction of tourists' interests, since the latter were their end consumers. Taking into account the growing demand for tourist product as a complex of coordinated (in time, location and order) tourist services, emergence and further rapid growth of tour operators as well as their quick transition to being the core business of tourist TNCs seem to be quite understandable.

Besides restructuring of interrelations inside corporations, tourist TNCs of the second generation turned to the production of various additional services for their clients – tourists using the services within their vertically integrated businesses. Thus, tourist TNCs got their first car rentals, specialized media, own productions of tourist-related commodities (suitcases and travel bags, photocamera accessories etc.). Logically enough, as the continuation of the same trend, with time, tourist TNCs also started providing their own insurance and other financial services (including travel loans, travel checks etc.).

Tourist TNCs of the third generations were already the corporations with quite explicitly dominating role of tour operating and agents' network. Moreover, large enough tour operators, which previously were present at the transnational level of business thanks to their inclusion into international hotel and transport business, became now capable enough for independent transnationalization. Transition to this new form of tourist TNCs became possible not only due to better financial condition of many tourist enterprises worldwide, but more due to the increased interest to this business from the side of both private and institutional investors. Early 1990s already witnessed the increased attention to the intangible resources of tour operators, including their brands, availability of constant client base, well-developed agent network. These factors guaranteed success for nearly any investment project within international tourism.

During the same 1990s tour operating became independently transnational sort of business, almost fully independent from hotel chains and transport enterprises. Now tour operators were able to set new directions and destinations and use their own tools of transnationalization to conquer new markets. Intensive development of information technologies in the same period made it possible to set sufficient connections between numerous offices worldwide along with numerous suppliers. In parallel to that, economic globalization was gradually turning to be a cultural phenomenon too, thus increasing the international cost of tourist brands manifold. Cultural globalization was also one of the major reasons for another boom in demand for mass, standardized tours, now in both developed and developing countries. These mass tours made tour operators the key player in tourism TNCs' functioning.

Since late 1980s transnational tourism business stretched its expansionary tentacles also on suppliers. Motivation to increase own competitiveness on the global scale, basing on lower prices and guaranteeing good quality at the same time, stimulates larger tour operators to acquire hotel and transport companies. This means tour operators tend to demonstrate top-down (or downstream, in other words) growth. Same trend, interestingly, has been also peculiar for many transnational industrial enterprises. This sort of expansion allows tour operators have minimum expenses on tourist services' production thanks to numerous extra opportunities provided by transnationalization, including transfer pricing, more efficient tax planning, business processes' optimization etc. Moreover, exclusion of independent intermediaries (mostly suppliers) means more guarantees that tourist services will be provided timely and at the needed level of quality. Also, transnational tour operator gets additional advantages from stability growth under the conditions of multifactor dynamics of the tourist market development. To some extent, transnational tour operators could be even treated as truly independent economic agents of the global level.

Tourist TNCs of the third generation had the following key distinctive features:

- They viewed the market and own competitive position on the planetary level;

- They did their research and had profound knowledge on the key competitors and the possible methods to be used in the global competitive fight;

- They were operating either on the global scale, or at least on the level of truly large regions;

- They were using a significant share from their profits on research, first of all technological one, and also on HR development and supply for all their activities;

- All their branches and representative offices were coordinated using the most advanced information technologies;

- Each production within a TNC was organized in the most flexible way, its structure and methods being easily adapted to the constantly changing conditions of international production;

- All enterprises and branches are closely united within the common international network of management;

- There are integration agreements with other TNCs, also operating in the sector of tourist services' production.

Therefore, tourist TNCs of the third generation should be described, first of all, through the prism of the leading role belonging to tour operators and tour agents. Also, tour operators' expansion into the hotel businesses and transport sector should be taken into account (and this should be understood as related diversification of business activities).

Transition to yet another generation of tourist TNCs was connected with the spread of non-related diversification, which gradually became one of the key strategies of transnational companies operating in the sector in question. This non-related diversification usually meant that a parent company was buying some totally different types of businesses, with hardly any connection to tourism. This expansion of tourist TNCs on other types of economic activities was caused, on the one hand, by their stronger economic stand overall and their enormous financial capacities (putting it simply, they were able to sign nearly any M&A deal, regardless the sector). On the other hand, expansion was caused by the growing independence of tourist TNCs from the world markets' fluctuations which indirectly determined the state of tourism in regions and also globally.

The prominent role in all business activities of the TNCs' fourth generation belongs to banks and other financial institutions. The latter have become a mandatory element within the structure of any TNC which has international transactions, especially if this TNC plans to perform M&A, engage in leasing, crediting or investment activities.

Tourism TNCs which have already become global are engaged in implementation of the strategy of large groups' formation. These groups unite production, trade/retail and financial companies. Apart from having strategic economic alliances between themselves, TNCs also strive to strengthen their cooperation with small and medium-sized business, both at home and abroad. In particular, they tend to widen their networks of suppliers and providers by means of adding small firms which are quite successful when it comes to new technologies' introduction in tourism services' production. These smaller firms are often able to develop independently new types of tourist product and perform their promotion. These firms are also strong enough to maintain their own material and technical basis etc. This multibranch network of subcontracts enables tourist TNCs free themselves from many minor (or not really financially meaningful) operations and functions, and thus − concentrate on the most prospective directions which often require significant volumes of investment too.

According to Peter F. Drucker *(1966)* the leading American specialist in efficient management, the future belongs to the enterprises of medium size (from 200 to 400 employees). Such enterprises are small enough to remain flexible, and at the same time they are large enough for serious investments in own innovations and their implementation. Following roughly the same logic, tourism TNCs, in parallel to ongoing enlargement and diversification of activities, reject the idea of gigantomania in their productions. Thus, we can observe that the size of production units within a corporation tends to reduce, while specialization of these production units is getting narrower. In the opinions of A. Mikhailushkin and P. Shimko *(2005),* TNCs are "losing their weight", that is, they are becoming less cumbersome, at the same time, they are "developing muscles" − that is, they are becoming much stronger due to higher flexibility and better maneuverability.

This fourth generation of tourist TNCs also become active participants of numerous deals on mergers and acquisitions, noteworthy, not as objects of these deals, but as immediate buyers. These M&As also get a new direction – not traditional downstream, as it used to be when TNCs got the right to manage their key suppliers. Now after a M&A deal the TNC gets the right to manage new types of businesses, with their direct and immediate effect on the suppliers' performance. Consequently, TNCs themselves became the macrofactors within the external environment of the tourism sector.

TO SUM UP

In the middle of the 20th century transnationalization of tourism business was caused, first of all, by the imperfections of the still forming international tourism market. Large enterprises, driven by the growth of demand for international tourist trips and functioning under the conditions of already tight competition at national markets, were forced to move to the transnational level of management with the aim to overcome the influence of such market bottlenecks as national barriers for free international trade in tourist services due to significant differences in economic, social, political, cultural, religious conditions of people's lives in different countries. Another bottleneck was related to differences between various national taxation and currency exchange regimes as well as differences in costs behind the attraction of various factors into tourist service production. Thus, the scale effect from tourist service production was seen as the means to achieve additional competitive advantages. Moreover:

- Transnationalization of tourism business started in the middle of the 20th century, thus already then with about a 50-year delay from industrial and agricultural productions;

- Among the causes for this delay we need to mention, first of all, later (than in other sectors) development of the world market, later transition of tourism into an international, then also global and mass phenomenon as well as lower investment attractiveness of foreign tourism objects due to significant potential costs of such investment projects and their narrow specialization on provision of tourist services only;

- Transnationalization of international tourism started with the emergence of hotel chains and transport companies due to the fact that these companies had (and still have) high-cost material and technical base which could have been easily resold in case of any risk;

- Foreign direct investments in the hotel business and transportation was limited for a long time, first of all, by limited opportunities for switching the specialization of tangible assets in case of an investment project's failure and its following resale. Another limitation was due to the necessity for simultaneous development of the existing hotel/transportation business in its several directions so that to reach higher efficiency from transnational tourist activity;

- For the hotel and transportation sectors themselves international tourism later became an additional stimulus for further transnationalization, since tourism sector, in the middle of the 1980s, became a truly mass phenomenon, mainly due to wide spread of franchising mechanisms in it, which managed to lower the entry barriers at international tourism markets and also to minimize many risks related to transnational activities;

- Transnationalization of tourism business was covering primarily the most developed countries of the Western world. Inclusion of developing economies into these transnational processes took place slightly later, with more rapid development of transport and communications, and also due to the fact that intercontinental tourism became much more real for the many;

- The subsector of tour operators and agents entered the stage of transnationalization much later. This is because key assets of both operators and agents are mostly of intangible nature, while investors, including big international investors, started paying attention to intangible assets (such as brand or new advanced technologies, for example) quite later, mostly in the last two decades of the previous century;

- The current stage in transnationalization of tourism business demonstrates that the leading role already belongs to the tour operators which are financially most stable. Moreover, they have quite easy access to financial resources of the largest banks since the latter are often also very much interested in further enlargement of both tourist and hotel TNCs which often happens through mergers and acquisitions. As of today, the leading role at the world tourism market belongs to American and European tourism TNCs.

Chapter 3

CONTEMPORARY CONDITIONS FOR TOURISM SECTOR TRANSNATIONALIZATION

ABSTRACT

Dynamics of the contemporary stage in transnationalization of tourism and hospitality sectors is predetermined by the specificity of sector's overall development, its placement in one of the four stages of the sector's consolidation process which, in its turn, predetermines the national tourism's capacities to implement efficient strategies of expansion onto foreign markets as well as the rate of tourism sector's attractiveness for potential foreign investors. The third chapter considers the organizational peculiarities of international M&A processes in the tourism sector and analyzes the instruments used in assessment of their economic efficiency. Also, consolidation of tourism industries from different countries is studied as the factor influencing the sectoral dynamics of transnationalization processes.

International expansion and other preconditions for prosperity at the international tourism market

The very end of the 1990s as well as first years of the new century witnessed quite a significant number of mergers and acquisitions among huge international companies. These deals have changed the face of many sectors and many national economies too, both developed and developing. These radical corporate transformations were taking place on the background of profound changes in the production processes in parallel to gradual establishment of new information economy in developed countries and ongoing globalization processes.

From the purely economic standpoint, most of M&A deals can be explained from the standpoint of desire to increase the volume of property, grow profits and guarantee certain return rates on the invested capital (the latter, as a rule, is manifested through aggregate shareholder value of a company). The core specific feature of such deals is that this aim is reached not by means of own development and use of internal managerial, financial, production and distribution capacities. The very mechanism of mergers and acquisitions is usually applied when it is quite possible to obtain competitive advantages under much lower costs directly due to participation of external sources, that is, by means of acquiring assets of other companies.

Essentially, the process of mergers and acquisitions as the circulation of assets can be understood as the mechanisms redistributing property from less efficient owners to more efficient ones, or as the process of company's management reassignment following the best interests of owners – from less efficient managers to more efficient ones, with the key aim of increasing both profits and incomes from the capital invested. The growth of company's cost in this case would mean its growing competitiveness which, in its turn, causes higher credit rank, additional investment opportunities, expansion and/or diversification of production, more intensive R&D, entry to new markets etc.

In the middle of the 1990s the tourism business reached a certain level of development which was described by overall high sectoral indicators of profitability and active growth dynamics. This, in its turn, caused more live interest on the side of investors to tourism enterprises. And this more intensive interest of investors, in turn, meant that entry barriers at many related regional and also global markets became quickly and significantly higher. The level of competition among tourism TNCs, high costs of marketing programs at tourism market, even higher costs for real estate, strengthening role of intangible assets in tourist services' production – all these factors had their positive influence on the growth of expenditures, which were necessary for enterprises while entering local and/or international tourist markets. Growth of entry barriers, including those related to time factor (the effect from a particular tourist market entry was taking force later and later, thus requiring significant time spending on its own organization), only increased the attractiveness of M&A deals, since one of the key outcomes from the latter was the fact that the involved corporation became able to step over a certain entry barrier and also get additional stimuli for further growth from the merged external unit.

Many tourism companies that opted for expansion and/or diversification faced the inevitable question concerning their own way to conquer new markets. Most of them had to choose between two alternatives: to develop own production or to buy out (merge) the already existing enterprise. And many of them opted for the second alternative between these two *(World Investment Report, 2016)*. However, advantages obtained from quick entry to a new market and/or getting know-hows in a specific field (or at a particular market) are often accompanied by numerous risks closely related to this alternative: two thirds of all mergers turn out to be loss-making at the end, thus leading to later resale of the acquired company or even shutdown of the whole business as such *(Marrying in haste, 2000)*.

In the middle of the 20th century one of the key stimuli for M&A deals was potential reduction of transportation spending, however, the later wave of M&As at the end of the 1990s was already preconditioned by the lowering cost of telecommunications as well as by other achievements in the field of IT development. After reaching a certain size any tourism-sector TNC became too slow in its operations and information exchange in particular, and this obviously hindered its growth and further development overall. While after the emergence and active spread of electronic commerce and paperless offices the borders for further growth became significantly wider. Cheaper and more efficient at the same time communications enabled companies allocate their productions at various countries maintaining at the same time all necessary organizational contacts and vital information for direct management of all business processes at the local level.

Numerous research studies on the phenomenon of M&As *(for example, Savchuk, 2002; Konina, 2005)* suggest a range of very different motives of companies behind such deals.

Taking into account that the key motive of tourist TNCs in this case is profit maximization, all motives can be divided into the following groups:

1.   Aiming at lowering spending (financial one, first of all).

2.   Aiming at increasing/stabilizing incomes.

3.   Neutral motives.

In its generalized form, classification of motives for mergers and acquisitions in international tourism is presented in Table 3.1.

Table 3.1. Structure of key motives behind mergers/acquisitions of companies

Lowering expenses	Neutral motivation	Increasing incomes
Scale effect	Company's value growth	Diversification
Centralization of functions	Corporation reaching super-size	More chances for monopolization
Eliminating the doubling of functions	Personal motivations of particular managers	Higher creditworthiness
Overcoming inefficiency	Protection from being merged	More opportunities to get larger orders and better contracts
Joint R&D		Access to new information
Cheaper access to information		
Lower costs of crediting		
Easier tax load (optimization and tax planning)		

Apart from motives for mergers and acquisitions, there are also the so-called platforms – common, for the two merging enterprises, principles of doing business. Presence of such common platforms is the key precondition for a synergy effect from a merger/acquisition, since availability of such a platform usually means a leapfrogging growth of efficiency in all production activities. Joint exploitation of the platform, mutual exchange of technologies between two integrating business are the key guarantees for the synergy effect.

On the other hand, availability of a platform for mergers and acquisitions, first of all, reduces the barriers in the course of integration. Secondly, it significantly narrows the time gap between the end of integration and the emergence of synergy effect. Companies being united on the basis of such a platform manage to adapt to each other much quicker, while the very process of their unification becomes less painful and does not cause the need in thorough restructuring of both already existing and joint businesses.

In the process in closing M&A deals in tourism business the core is formed by client, technological, production, financial, managerial and marketing platforms.

Client platform as the basis for mergers and acquisitions in tourism assumes there is an open opportunity for simultaneous use of the enlarged client database of the merging enterprises in the course of their, now joint, activities. Taking into account that the initiator of a M&A deal in this case is a tourist enterprise, we can easily imagine the profile and the specificity of the second company – the one being merged. Their services may be aimed at satisfying the demands of the same clients. This also means they can mutually exchange their client databases attracting the clients of each other. For example, a tourist company specializing in servicing large corporate clients, may buy out an exhibition center or a business hotel somewhere downtown. Such a hotel would have several conference halls and rooms and thus would be able to provide event management services. Another example: a retail trade enterprise (a supermarket network) can acquire a network of tourist agencies, all offering cheap package tours to the most popular destinations of mass tourism. Further exchange of client databases of these integrated companies may contribute to the synergy effect from their joint work.

The key feature of a technological platform used for mergers and acquisitions in tourist services production concerns the commonness of technologies used by integrated companies in the course of their production activities. For example, a hotel network can increase the efficiency of using its own corporate system of online booking by means of consolidating this system with the system of airline tickets booking. Such consolidation is quite possible and is also technically relatively easy to perform due to the fact that technologies of clients' servicing in tourism overall, hospitality and transportation in particular, are almost identical (especially when it comes specifically to booking).

A common production platform in M&A deals assumes there is one common basis for integration of production processes' interdependencies of the merging enterprises. In other words, integrating businesses often have well-established client-partner relations or contracting relations which make them mutually dependent from each other in terms of production processes' efficiency.

For example, performance of a tourist agency is in direct and strong dependence from the professionalism of an advertisement agent. At the same time, this tourist agency may be the most important client for an advertisement agency. And this mutual dependence creates a production platform for their future potential consolidation. In the hospitality sector quite similar relations may emerge, for example, between a hotel and a construction company, especially if the latter guarantees appropriate conditions of the material basis of this hotel enterprise or promises construction of similar new hotels in other regions. Any hotel, actually, may establish this sort of relations with a wide range of enterprises from other sectors: with agricultural producers, who are supplying products for further catering in the hotel; with other enterprises – providing utility services, transportation etc.

In the field of tourist transportation in particular a common production platform may exist between transportation companies on the one side and producers of transportation means on the other (aircraft construction companies, producers of large buses usually used in tourism, constructors of cruise liner) or enterprises responsible for organization of passengers' delivery (airports, railway stations etc.).

Financial platform for mergers and acquisitions at the tourism market assumes that one company has either sufficient financial resources, or stable access to financing along with sophisticated instruments for smart financial (and first of all tax) planning, while another company – the object of a merger/acquisition – does not have sufficient enough volumes of such resources at its disposal. For example, a cause for merger/acquisition can be one tourist enterprise having tax preferences, while another is having significantly larger financial flows (larger volumes of sales and thus higher incomes) *(Ushakov at al., 2017b)*. This means that the latter would sooner or later have the desire (and intention) to lower its tax payments. In this example the financial platform for a merger is formed by availability of financial resources at one enterprise and catastrophic lack of these resources at the other.

Managerial platform for tourist M&As rests on the identical corporate requirements to managers of the middle and top levels at both companies. That is, there must be some sort of confirmation that managers of the merging companies are capable of joint activities within the same organizational structure (which includes managers' rotation in some cases) without any damage for efficient functioning of both companies. Availability of such a managerial platform for mergers and acquisitions of tourist/hotel enterprises is able to reduce the barriers related to retraining of managers and/or recruitment of external specialists at foreign labour markets *(Kirillov et al, 2017)*.

And finally, marketing platform of the merging enterprises rests on unity and/or identity of the market behavior strategies, and not only in relation to their target audience, but also in relation to the core instruments of promotion, their own brands, channels for getting feedback from clients, loyalty programs etc. This marketing platform forms the basis for further consolidation of efforts in already joint marketing activities. The latter often includes rebranding since one brand acquires another or because coexistence of brands requires certain revision.

Table 3.2. Platforms for mergers and acquisitions in the tourism sector

	Platform	Objects for potential M&As
TOUR OPERATORS	Marketing/ Client-oriented	Tour agencies; hotel chains; exhibition companies; car rentals; transportation companies; retail chains; e-commerce enterprises; publishing houses; mass media
	Production	Hotels; construction companies; public utilities; enterprises producing means of transportation; agricultural suppliers; advertisement businesses; recruiting agencies and retraining companies; gas stations and other suppliers of fuels; global electronic systems of booking; real estate agencies; cargo delivery and other logistics enterprises
	Financial	financial consulting and other financial services; insurance companies
	Technological	Software producers; Internet companies; IT-related training centers; specialized education institutions, including universities and separate faculties
	Managerial	Enterprises of the service sector; hotel chains; box offices; retail trade enterprises

Apart from all these, rather predictable platforms for mergers and acquisitions, an alternative platform can be also the "support" from national governments: any company which has some sort of informal connections with authorities is automatically more interesting as an object of a potential merger, and it also can become the initiator of an integration process as well. At the same time support for particular tourist enterprises by state authorities may take very different forms – from stare orders for various business services provision (in tourism sector this can be, for example, various social tourism projects) to direct lobbying of tourism corporations' interests.

Sectoral consolidation: reserves for further growth and the factor of international stability

Tourism and hotel industries in various regions of the world are consolidated to a various degree and extent, and these degree and extent are predetermined primarily by the level of a particular region's engagement in international tourist flows, and also by the export orientation of a particular region or the state overall. The degree of regional tourist market consolidation, in its turn, determines the aims of all further mergers and acquisitions, assigning various tourism companies different roles - either that of a merger subject, or an object.

In the states with huge tourism market potential (high paying capacity of local population, high enough demand for both foreign and local trips, free access to various information sources related to tourism etc.) the tourism sector would be consolidated to its very maximum. Such markets are usually dominated by large transnational companies which are specializing in mass production of tourism services, therefore, growth in the number of M&As at these markets would be rather complicated (since the market limits are already quite visible, entry barriers become quite high).

However, there is a way out of this situation which is often used by the representatives of transnational tourism business. This would be the strategy of expansion onto foreign tourism markets (usually targeting the countries the tourism sector of which is consolidated to a much less extent). Another potential direction for further expansion of the already large business would be conglomerative mergers and acquisitions within national borders of a base country.

In the process of decision-making concerning foreign expansion transnational tourism companies consider, most frequently, two possible variants: either buying out a foreign company at a consolidated market (though the level of consolidation must be lower than at home), or invest own assets into a relatively new foreign enterprise functioning at a regional tourist market and being at an early stage of consolidation.

The first of these two strategies has one highly important advantages - buying out a company at the already consolidated market is usually a quick process (provided integration into the parent company is efficient). Secondly, one may expect sufficiently high dividends quite soon since the merged tourism business is already well organized, is stably present at the local market and is also demonstrating a range of other obvious competitive advantages. On the other hand, implementation of this strategy is quite costly since entry barriers at such market are very high. Even though barriers are lower than at the domestic (for the investor) tourism market, they are still high enough to require serious capital investments. In such cases, ideal conditions are formed for the so-called megadeals: when huge and known companies from the countries - leaders in tourism business consolidation, acquire large local companies which are functioning under the conditions of less consolidated tourism markets.

Analysis of regional tourism markets in developed countries allows us making a conclusion that today the maximum level of the tourism sector consolidation is demonstrated by Germany and the USA. These two leaders are followed, with a significant gap inbetween though, by France and the UK.

According to expert estimations, the annual turnover at German tourist market (the largest in Europe) is around 27 bln USD. About one third of these huge German pie belongs to TUI (Tourism Union International), smaller slices belong to NUR (Neckermann and

Reising) and LTU (noteworthy here: in Europe overall the latter two companies are ranked the third and the fourth accordingly). These three leaders of German market together control more than 70% of its overall revenues.

Throughout the 1990s more than 12 thousand German tour agents out of 17 thousand (their overall number in the country) were in contact, to some degree, with TUI. However, in order to go beyond national borders and conquer global space this company needed a solid and generous investor. This was German steel concern Preussag AG. Prior to that, this steel giant had already bought a group of transportation companies Hapag Lloyd (cargo and cruise fleet, charters). Thus, the final combination was merging the enormous transportation capacities of Hapag Lloyd with huge tourist database of TUI. This newly emerged alliance of a successful tour operator with a no less successful transportation company was literary unbeatable. Thus, quite soon TUI managed to outpace the key competitor - NUR company.

In Germany most of tour operators gradually turned into huge multifunctional conglomerates, while in the UK tour operators remained engaged only in tourism and transportation services. In England tour operating concept was known back in the 19th century already, and now UK became the largest producer of standardized tour packages in the world, hitting the target of 10 mln sales a year.

At the beginning of the 1990s all large tour operators of Great Britain were involved in a severe fight for market shares. As a result, the end prices for their packages reached the minimum possible level. Price wars among British tour operators had actually started back in the late 1970s already, however, only in the second half of the 1990s they reached their peak, causing much instability at the tourism market. Due to these wars the very structure of the sector changed radically. In 1993 the average profit level in British tourism was no more than 5%, while the largest tour operators that managed to survive in the price war (Thomson and Airtours) had their profits on the level of merely 4%. Owners Abroad company had even less - about 2% only. However, in 1994 Thomson controlled about 34% of the whole market, while Owners Abroad (the name was changed to

First Choice in the same year) had 12%. Airtours covered 18% of the market, and Cosmos had 7%. Taken together, all these companies provided around 70% of all tour packages in the United Kingdom *(here and after data from RATA-news)*.

The largest UK tour operator (and one of the largest in the whole world) is Thomson Holidays, it belongs to the Canadian group Thomson Corp. Back in 1992 this company was second largest in Europe, having the annual turnover of 1,623 mln ECU. The company was founded in 1965 by an independent British operator SkyTours. Later it was acquired by Canadian intermediary group Thomson Corp along with the charter airline company British Airways. Later on, this company was merged with three other UK tour operators - Riviera Holidays, Gaytours and Luxe-tours. Thus, Thomson Skytours emerged. In 1972, after acquiring the group of tour agencies Lunn Polly, the company got another name - Thomson Holidays. During a decade (1984 to 1994) it managed to increase the overall number of its agencies tenfold. The number of agencies was 500 at the end of this period, while the quantity of personnel was over 2800.

In 1988 Thomson Holidays signed a truly unprecedented contract, according to which it was buying out Horizon Holidays, even though first the approval of the anti-monopoly committee was required. At that time Horizon Holidays was third largest tour operator in the UK (after Thomson Holidays itself and then ILG - International Leisure Group). At the time of this buying out Horizon Holidays owned quite attractive assets: Wings - the tour operator specializing in long-term vacationing; OSL - the villas rental services; GSA - the network of clubs for family leisure, and finally the charter airline Orion.

Today Thomson Holidays has three core structural units - Thomson Touroperation, British Airways and Lunn Polly. Already back in 1994 these three units were the largest key players in their specific subsectors of tourism activities.

Thomson Holidays acquiring of Horizon was actually provoked by severe competition - that of ILG. In 1988 the difference between market shares was really insignificant: Thomson Holidays controlled

29,3% of the market, ILG had 24,8%, while Horizon got 12%. After the merger, Thomson got an obviously larger share, however, since all tour operators were forced to drop the prices during the 1990s, the common merged share decreased gradually to 30% (from about 40% initially). At the same time, Thomson Holidays managed to increase the average price per one client by 17%, thus still increasing the overall profits. Very soon ILG was forced to leave the market as such, thus making Thomson the obvious leader and winner of the British market. On this background, Lunn Polly and British Airways served as auxiliary companies.

French sector of tour operating was consolidated to a much lesser extent than in other European countries. 300 French companies operating in this sector together had about 20 ths employees, serving about 1,5 mln clients a year. The key tour operators included: Club Mediterrians, Nouvelle Frontier, Soter, Framme, Luc Voyage and Pacce. However, the share of top-3 companies taken together was no more than 30% of the national market (while first two British companies, for example, covered over 60% of their market at that time). French tour operators were very much interested in vertical integration, with airlines in the first place. For example, in 1993 Air France acquired the tour operator Go Voyages, while Air Inter already had its own tour operator - TFI. In a similar manner but slightly later CorsAir merged with Nouvelle Frontier, and Air Liberte - with Luc Voyage.

Low (as compared to the UK and Germany) level of tourism sector consolidation in France was compensated by the presence of well-developed hotel networks, the largest of which being Accor.

In other European countries the market of tourist packages was under the control of a few operators. For example, in Switzerland such companies as Kuoni, Hotelplan, Airtour and Imhog together were doing more than 70% of all sales.

In Sweden the total share of Vigressor, Atlas, Space and Rezo was also over 70%. Top-2 tour operators in the Netherlands - GIT and Arke Reisen - together covered over 50% of the market.

However, considering the relatively low volumes of sales of all these tour operators due to rather limited capacities of the related national markets as such, we cannot really state that these leaders of the national tourism markets can be automatically considered the key players of the global tourism market.

Among the largest hotel networks in Europe we need to mention the Spanish chain Sol Melia and the Scandinavian Rezidor SAS.

International tourism in the US and Canada was primarily oriented on the Carribeans, and also Latin America and some of European countries. Today more than 2000 tour operators are serving the US clients, which is more than 3,5 larger than their number back in the 1970s. The largest tour operators at the American market are American Express, Thomas Cook, Caravan Tours, Gatney Holidays. In Canada the leaders in tour operating are Canadien Pacific and Tour Montroyal. However, 70% of all tourist packaged offers are actually internal - to California, Florida or Hawaii etc. Due to extremely severe competition at the American market of tour operating the maximum possible level of profit there is around 3%.

The key players at today's tourism market of the US and Canada are the hotel chains once merged with other large tourist enterprises, such as with transportation companies, for example (Cendant Corp, Choice Hotels International (CHH), Best Western International (BWI), Six Continents Hotels (SCH), Marriott International Inc. (MII), Hilton Hotels Corporation and some others).

Analysis of the consolidation degree for the tourism and hotel markets in developed countries allows us classify them according to the share and the presence of large business at a particular market and also according to the volumes of sales demonstrated by the largest tourism companies and hotel chains (see Table 3.3).

Table 3.3. -Classification of tourism and hotel markets in developed countries

The share of large businesses at the market	The volumes of sales	
	Small	Large
Small	Spain, Greece, Portugal	Great Britain, France, Japan
Large	Switzerland, Netherlands, Sweden, Italy, Canada	Germany, USA

Separately we need to consider the states of the so-called "catching-up development" of their tourism sectors. They have emerged on the world map of tourism relatively recently, and their key feature is the dominating orientation on the export of tourist services' production.

Tourism sector in these countries is young but developing very dynamically. Here we first of all speak about third-world countries which are striving to participate in the world trade in every way possible. Their national production is mostly export-oriented, while their internal market is quite small, moreover, the paying capacity of their local population is very low, thus, this population cannot demonstrate enough demand for tourism development.

Therefore, national tourism industries in these countries are largely export-oriented, that is, concentrated on satisfying the tourism demand of population from developed countries. Own population of these countries does not have enough material and/or financial resources for active consumption of the already available tourist product. Moreover, for the locals tourism as such is some sort of unattainable luxury. On the other hand, this local population is actively employed by the tourism sector.

Countries with the catching-up tourist markets usually have highly differentiated social structure in terms of population incomes. Moreover, in all these countries human potential is usually poorly developed, and there is also the whole long list of various social problems (with healthcare services' provision, criminality, sanitation and epidemiological control etc.). At the same time, certain territories within these countries are still attractive for global tourists since they still have unique tourist resources and are relatively safer than the rest of a country.

When there is an obvious lack of own financial resources and at the same time there is a clearly expressed global interest in local tourist resources - sooner or later foreign corporations would pour their investments into national tourism industry, and the latter would start developing quite rapidly. Low paying capacity of the internal market means all tourist enterprises would concentrate on the export of their products and services, thus, most of the resorts would soons specialize in welcoming foreigners. Eventually this nearly always leads to the emergence of the so-called "tourist reservations" - these are small territories with excellent infrastructure and very limited access for local population (apart from those being actually employed there).

Thus, rapidly developing tourism sector in these countries is mostly specializing in beach resort tourism and various leisure activities which do not require significant capital investments, while their competitive advantages are directly correlated with the attractiveness of a particular tourism venue in general *(Ushakov, 2006)*.

These tourist markets are vaguely consolidated and/or at the very initial stage of the consolidation process. At the moment we can assume that the Middle East countries, Northern Africa and South-East Asia are still at the initial stage of consolidation, while tourism markets of Turkey, Emirates, Eastern Europe and some of the Caribbean countries are already at the stage of active growth.

The major contribution into consolidation of tourism and hotel markets in developing countries belongs to tourism TNCs which are trying to activate their presence through the implementation of foreign investment projects (for example, expansion of American hotel chains on European countries; buying out other enterprises closely related to tourist services' provision; creation of joint companies etc.).

At the same time we have to admit that national tourism business at developing markets is not ready for consolidation at all: it lacks own funds, it does not have breakthrough technologies, it cannot boast having sufficient enough volumes of sales.

Tourist markets in developing countries still have low entry barriers which allow for the presence of a large number of small tourist agencies and hotels, the shares of which are really minor. Still, with every new year to come their common share is reducing due to active policies of Western corporations which are gradually pushing small local businesses out of the tourism sector, especially when it comes to welcoming foreigners. Western corporations entering these new for them markets already have at hand a whole range of competitive advantages which concern both production of tourist services and their further sale. These large foreign businesses are able to win at local markets primarily because they have direct access to rich consumer markets of developed countries (and tourists from these countries are the key clients for tourism sectors in developing countries).

At the same time, there is hardly any chance for a local tourism company of a host developing country to enter the tourist markets of the developed Western countries alone. Their entry barriers are too high for that, and there are no resources, even on the state level, for developing economies to overcome these barriers.

Another instrument used by Western TNCs to exclude local tourist enterprises from servicing foreign clients is the global spread of common quality standards. Small enterprises originating from developing economies are simply not able to afford this sort of compliance.

Let's take the global system of hotel enterprises' classification by "stars". Building a five-star hotel (according to European standards) using only the resource of local businesses in a developing state is not probable as such, even a country is relatively well developed.

Same unlikely would be provision of the already constructed hotel with the services of a similar level. Even a tourist firm alone would find it hard to find enough personnel to comply with the global quality standards, without sufficient investments from outside.

Therefore, tourist markets in developing countries find themselves in a rather ambivalent situation. On the one hand, there is a more profitable segment of foreign guests, it is more consolidated due to presence (which is growing all the time) of foreign tourist corporations. On the other hand, there is a less attractive segment of the tourism sector, servicing low-income internal (or regional) tourists and/or providing occasional tourism services to the first sector (e.g., transfers to/from airport/hotel, excursions etc.). This second segment is only at the initial stage of consolidation, it also has low entry barriers and a huge number of functioning enterprises. At the same time, there is no obvious leader or monopolist/oligopolists.

Therefore, it is quite clear that the more a country is engaged in international tourist flows (the more interesting it is for Western tourist corporations) - the more consolidated its national tourism sector would be.

Consequently, a developing tourism market usually has a two-level model. The upper level of this model is represented by a segment servicing foreign tourists but it also has several exits to local consumer markets due to the strong influence of transnational tourism corporations. To this level belong: transnational tourism corporations themselves, their local branches or their local representatives operating under franchising agreements (e.g., local hotels that are members of the international hotel chains).

The lower level of the sector is represented by national producers which cannot have direct access to foreign and/or international consumer markets, thus, they are doomed to service internal clients only or at best - clients from other developing countries. In this low-income subsector competitive fight becomes a real battle for survival: since entry barriers are initially very low, appearance of new competitors is unavoidable, moreover, often there is no obvious leader in sales' volumes. Thus, all competitors are forced to engage into price wars which, sooner or later, would harm their own financial condition limiting their future development prospects.

In case a particular tourist destination gains more popularity at the consumer markets of developed countries, its upper segment would be able to gain more volume by means of "borrowing" from the lower segment. Competitive fight between branches of Western corporations and small national companies seems to be simply impossible in the tourism sector.

And if internal tourism becomes more profitable - more frequent would become deals on M&A through buying out national tourist companies which has strong positions at the internal tourist market (for example, having a strong brand, a database of regular clients etc.). Here we consider the process of mergers and acquisitions in the context of tourist sector consolidation.

The most popular tourist destinations can be assigned their special places on the consolidation curve depending on their stage of development (see Figure 3.1).

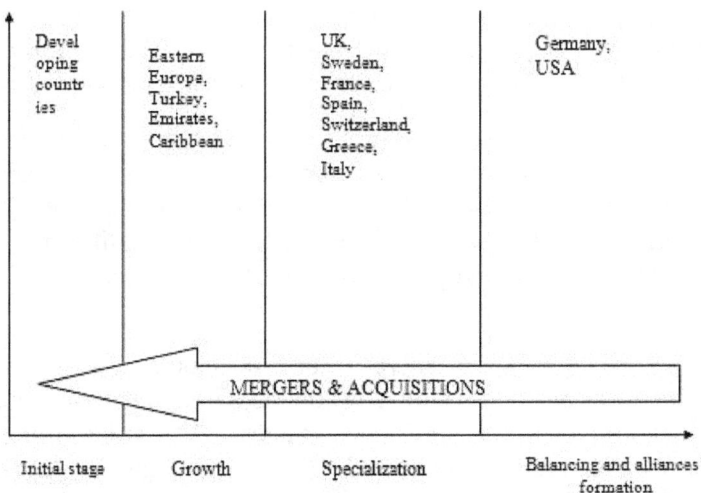

Figure 3.1. Various countries on the curve of tourism sector consolidation

On this figure above we can see not only the placement of various countries on the consolidation curve and who are the current leaders, but also the key direction in the ongoing processes of mergers and acquisitions at the global market of tourism (the arrow). It would be logical to assume that tourism sectors of the countries that are at more advanced stages of the consolidation process would pay more attention to M&A deals and to the opportunities to buy out the enterprises from less consolidated and thus less financially solid tourism sectors. It would be also obvious to assume that the smaller is the gap in consolidation of the tourism markets of the object company and the subject company (in relation to a potential M&A deal) - the higher would be the cost of this deal, and the effect from it would be visible much sooner.

Maximal activity of the M&A subjects would be demonstrated by German and American tourism businesses. On the other hand, of maximal interest as objects of potential international mergers and acquisitions would be companies operating in the tourism sectors of developing countries (they would be interesting, first of all, for the global leaders in tourism, such as USA, Germany, France, Italy, Switzerland etc.).

At this, policies and strategies of such deals' initiators - representatives of large tourism businesses - would significantly depend on the degree of a particular tourism sector consolidation.

When the companies initiate M&As in the tourism sectors with less degree of consolidation, they normally have lower expenses (partially due to the use of franchising schemes). However, in the long term they still have to invest, and quite significantly, into additional promotion and popularization of the merged business at a regional market.

Merging or acquiring an enterprise at a developing market usually takes the form of traditional expansion (as a horizontal merger), this is especially typical for larger hotel chains. Or it can be in the form of vertical integration, when a TNC gets the right to coordinate several key foreign suppliers of tourist services.

The latter is especially relevant for large European tour operators that are often the initiators of buying out foreign airlines, hotels, excursion firms etc. In such a way tour operators guarantee themselves competitive positions at the international tourism market.

At the very end of the 1990s large retails companies also became objects of mergers initiated by tourism businesses. This was first of all applicable to large retail networks operating in countries with dynamically developing tourism destinations.

Western TNCs were purchasing national tour operators from developing countries in order to take use of their sales' volumes and brands' recognizability. Since consumer demand in developing economies was gradually growing, and more interest was demonstrated to both inbound and outbound international tourism, TNCs started using the bought out national tour operators to enter new for them and less consolidated markets. Such strategies were used, for example, at the markets of Eastern Europe and the CIS: Western corporations were entering these markets starting with a purchase of the already well-functioning national tour operator or of an agent network.

Expansion strategies of Western tourism corporations at less consolidated foreign markets were very much similar, if not identical. For example, TUI has several key strategies for conquering a new market. They usually start with increasing the tourists' inflow into a particular country, then this German company has several option to choose between. For example, it can buy out the control package of shares of the most obvious leader at the local market (as it was in the UK or in Turkey), or it can monopolize the market through franchising followed by the introduction of own (and highly efficient) system of corporate distribution.

Nearly always expansion of Western tourism corporation onto less consolidated developing market is accompanied by massive dumping, the key goal of which being complete extrusion of local tourist companies from the local market which is easily possible due to financial misbalance of powers in this fight.

Another group of M&As initiated by tourism corporations is represented by the deals signed at the already consolidated markets, often at the markets of these corporations' headquarters.

Mergers and acquisitions of tourist companies that are functioning at an already consolidated market form the grounds for the so-called mega-deals which cost billions of dollars. On the other hand, return from such deals is much quicker, if not instant, provided, of course, integration of a new business into the "older" organizational structure of the merging corporation is efficient enough.

Deals of this size usually have zero impact on consumer markets, actually. Trying to maximize the synergy effect from such a deal, the parent company would keep the brand of the merged company in operation and also would not intrude into its marketing strategy. Moreover, in many cases merging corporations in such cases do not even risk to implement serious HR changes. The world tourism practice actually knows the cases when the parent company, merging a much smaller company, was taking the brand name of the merged structure (for example, this was the case with C&N which bought out Thomas Cook in 1998).

At the end of the 1990s mergers and acquisitions at the already highly consolidated markets started to lead to the formation of the so-called conglomerates - when the initiating the deal company was collecting several types of businesses inside its own structure. And these businesses usually belonged to very much different sectors. This transition from horizontal mergers (when businesses were integrating because were similar, just functioning on different territories) and vertical mergers (when the core enterprise was merging with a supplier or with a provider of additional clients) to conglomerate types of mergers was quite logical overall and for tourism especially.

Any tourism company starts functioning as a small and, as a rule, specialized in something in particular enterprise with a rather limited choice of offers. In the course of its functioning and development this small company would obviously face the problem with the lack of funds and will also find itself vulnerable in the face of competition.

In most cases such companies are operating at the local tourism and/or hotel markets. Thus, their product is not competitive enough (neither in price, nor in quality) if compared with the "elder brothers" in the industry. Due to exactly the same reason during the first 3-5 years all efforts of such companies are focused on increasing the volumes of sales in own market segment and also on maximal widening of the client base *(Rudykh, 2005)*.

At this stage, the key source of enterprise financing would be reinvesting the early profits and also additional emission of securities.

If an enterprises managed to pass through this stage, sooner or later it will hit the niche "ceiling" due to its inability to expand further: at some point the sales' volume would get too stable and stop growing which means the company's share has reached its maximum.

At this moment top managers usually make the decision to start expansion, that is, to enter new markets, with the same product though (standardized, however, slightly corrected according to the regional specificity of a new market).

The company first moves from a regional market to a national one, then - from national to international one. However, even this international level of operations is not the final point in this journey. On the international level too the company may face the limit for further growth. At the tourist market this usually happens at the national level already, due to intense competition. And at this critical point of time the company makes up the decision to diversify.

There are two major ways to diversify production of services in tourism: to diversify the offer and to try to repeat the same stage in development but with a newer product now; or to turn to brand new types of activity which would not have obvious connection to the tourist services already being provided.

Majority of corporations in tourism, being at the early stages of their global rule, preferred related diversification, that is, they were offering a range of services "accompanying" tourist activities. But the stronger a corporation gets - the less time and efforts it needs to introduce a brand new product to a market under the good old brand. And the instruments of mergers and acquisitions which got widely spread during the 1990s only contributed to the efficiency of such strategies.

Still, even this state of affairs did not satisfy the appetites of many corporate top managers, turning them to the idea of conglomerate unions.

When the capacities and the organizational structure of a tourism corporation become stronger than the market mechanisms themselves, top management decides to perform the first conglomerate merger, thus pushing the parent company to the new frontiers of presence. The key reason behind this decision is usually the desire to redistribute most efficiently the accumulated (and huge) financial assets between several very different types of production activities.

The key preconditions for conglomerate integration of tourism corporations at the edge between 20th and 21st centuries were as follows:

- exhaustion of opportunities for further internal development of corporations in the tourism sector, for which redistribution of resources between the already existing units within the same sector became economically senseless;

- emergence of new opportunities for the corporations to redirect their financial resources into new fields of business;

- tourism TNCs became more efficient than the market itself since now they had new redistribution mechanisms (including intersectoral ones) for their excessive financial flows. Also, these corporations had highly efficient internal business processes.

TO SUM UP

Nature and contents of the M&A deals carried out by tourism corporations depend, first of all, on the degree of a particular tourist market consolidation. If a market is highly consolidated the merger deal initiated by a tourism corporation would be oriented on the creation of conglomerate structures with a diversified portfolio of numerous businesses (not always interrelated with tourism). And if a market is less consolidated, mergers and acquisitions performed at it would simply follow traditional expansionary goals.

Chapter 4

Transnationalized tourism: hyper-advantages from global competitiveness

ABSTRACT

Due to synergy effects from transnationalization, corporation gets its own set of global competitive advantages which can be called using the prefix hyper- (which means, first of all, the global measure of these competitive advantages, that is, company's capacity to make use of them at any regional or world market; secondly, massive opportunities which these advantages provide for company's strategic and tactical activities; and thirdly, low probability that any small or mid-sized company would be able to get same or similar competitive advantages). Therefore, economic efficiency of any transnational corporation operating in the tourism sector can be viewed from the standpoint of 6H model. To these 6Hs belong: hyper-profit, hyper-competitiveness, hyper-presence, hyper-positioning, hyper-mobility and hyper-prospective.

In this chapter we will consider all these hyper-advantages of TNCs along with the sources of their origin.

Go transnational to ride the wave of multipliers

Hyper-profit of a tourism TNC depends, first of all, on the capacity of this corporation to concentrate, within own production process, the emerging effect from the tourism multiplier in its full volume.

Tourism multiplier appears when means, spent by tourists, are redistributed between the subjects of the related tourism market step by step - from the producer of an end tourism product to producers of tourist services as components of a tourist product (e.g., from a tour operator to its own hotel, transportation companies, restaurants and so on). However, here we need to keep in mind the exclusion (by tour operator) of a certain share, the size of which depends to this operator's desire to save funds (that is, the stronger is this desire - the smaller share of the fees paid by tourists moves to the second level - to suppliers of tourist services) *(Ushakov & Kharchenko, 2017)*.

In their turn, suppliers of tourists services also use their free will to redistribute the obtained funds further. Of course, paying their bills is in the top of their priorities (utilities, salaries, bills from suppliers). This means that any sum paid by a tourist is gradually decreasing (by the share every new subject involved finds to be necessary). Still, this sum, going down from tour operator to tourist service supplier and so on, creates profit at each of these stages. Let's assume that all subjects are equal in taking their share (0.25). Then, distribution of a sum spent by a tourist would look like as follows:

Tour operator –	1000 money units
Key supplier of a tourist service (hotel+transport+restaurant)	750 money units
Suppliers of the first level	375 money units
Suppliers of the second level	250 money units
Suppliers of the third level	187 money units

and so on

As a result, one thousand abstract money units would create several waves of additional profit for several groups of people, doing business in a same region. The overall sum of profit in this case will be closer to 3000 money units. Therefore, in this example the size of tourism multiplier is roughly equal to 3. Obviously, the more upper subjects are inclined to exclude from this process - the smaller will be the size of the multiplier effect.

In some cases there might be a situation when all spendings of a tourist are concentrated around one subject - tourism transnational corporation itself. And today it is often the case since many tourism TNCs already have, within their own structure, own tour operator, own network of tourist agents, own hotels and transportation companies, own excursion tours and catering. In this case financial flows between the levels of suppliers (traditionally: through tour agent to our operator and then to the immediate producers of a tourist product) in case it all happens within the same corporation would only be the flows between various structural units and departments of this corporation.

We need to mention here that this "wave of profits" created by tourists does not only contribute to financial stability at each level of tourist service production but also activates further demand - on goods and services provided at the lower level of suppliers. Thus, we can assume that the whole "wave of profit" actually stays within the same company. If we return to the presented above simple example of how a tourist spends 1000 money units and adapt this model to the context of any contemporary transnational corporation, we can clearly see that the total effect from the tourism multiplier (equal to 3, under this model) is attributed to the production process inside one participant of the tourist market. Simply put, this means that it is the transnational corporation, not the tour operator and not the tourist service suppliers operating at the regional level, that will accumulate the overall multiplier effect, without dividing it into shares (in the example above this would be 3000 money units in total).

Getting into the network structure of a TNC these 1000 money units spent by a tourist on purchasing the tourist product will thus lead to the growth of intracorporate demand which would be several times higher than the initial spending of a consumer. This, in its turn, will create an additional economic incentive for further transnational tourist activities. Multibranch and differentiated structure of a tourist TNC serves here to get the maximum of possible outcomes from this multiplier effect.

In this context, diversification of activities carried out by a tourism TNC would be nearly always directed at merging not only directly related types of enterprises (hotels, transportation companies, catering, tour operators etc.), but also those indirectly dependant from tourism though potentially still useful for tourists (car rentals, insurance companies, shops with photo cameras and other equipment). To the same category may also belong much larger businesses, also indirectly related to tourism (construction firms, advertising agencies etc.).

This targeted diversification of the majority of today's tourism TNCs is yet another proof that contemporary large business has very little desire to share profits obtained from tourists through purchasing tourist products from outside, usually smaller companies. This means TNCs in tourism are doing their best to reach the maximum effect from tourism multiplier, accumulating it in a parent company.

Managing the multiplier effect in such a way, transnational corporations get an additional opportunity to increase their financial indicators, by means of circulating assets, first of all. And this becomes their key source of hyper-profit.

Go transnational! and other strategies of permanent income

The second important source of hyper-profit for corporations in the tourism sector is their capacity to implement, in parallel or in a certain order, various efficient strategies for own development *(Ushakov, 2016)*. All of these strategies are aimed to maximization of profitability from production activities. Contemporary management science distinguishes between several models of profit generation, the implementation of which requires spending a certain amount of company's resources, and not only material/financial ones, but also time resources and marketing skills. Transnational corporations operating in the tourism sector usually have a range of own advantages in all of these strategies. Thus, they are able to quickly direct profit in such a way so that to relocate the company to the so-called "permanent income zone".

The first of these strategic models is aimed at stabilization of company's profits and is based on consumer decisions. According to this strategy, a company carries out targeted investment, studying the consumer demand, and on the basis of the obtained information it makes decisions which are supposed to develop consumer relations further. At the first stages of this process implementation a company would naturally experience losses, however, later on, its profit will stabilize at a much higher level. Adapting this model of the enterprise transition to the "profit zone" to the context of tourism sector operations, we can outline several advantages TNCs are having as compared to small and mid-sized businesses in this regard. For example, corporations can be more relaxed in terms of strategy timing. Transnational corporation, with its solid financial and marketing resources, can allow itself spend much more time to going through the initial (unprofitable) stages in this model, thus doing more detailed research of consumer decisions and preferences.

A good example of a tourist company applying this model is Kuoni (Zurich, Switzerland). Its base strategy applied by several structural departments is investing in consumer. This corporation spent really a lot at the first stage of the cycle so that to collect the fullest possible data and reconsider how clients are spending their time. After that, Kuoni has redesigned its product in such a way so that it would fully comply to consumer demand. In such a way their corporate product has become an integral part of many operations performed by consumers. At the beginning of this process Kuoni experiences significant losses due to massive spending on focused marketing research and further marketing impact. However, after several months already this company was getting profit, inter alia, through cutting costs on consumer relations and increased consumer loyalty.

Another option is the model based on the product pyramid formation. Its most vital aspect is satisfying consumer preferences on separate parameters of the tourist product (time of servicing, quality of servicing, geography of destination options etc.). This pyramid rests on mass cheap tourist product, and the top of this pyramid is represented by more expensive tours with an individual approach. The larger part of corporate profit is actually concentrated on the top, however, the basis serves as the protecting brand shield and it also plays a strategically important role - it does not let all other competitors reach the top of the pyramid.

This strategy of reaching the "profit zone" may help reach many other strategic goals too, however, it does not allow for the growth in parallel to the welfare growth of clients or in parallel to the key competitors' growth. Thus, some of the clients with low or middle (but growing) income may gradually become more loyal to a closest competitor.

Growing welfare of the client base (for example, due to their ageing and/or career development) may provoke the closest competitors to be more active, to increase the quality of their offers, to provide more individualized and original tours. This means that such competitors will start threatening the top of the corporate product pyramid. To prevent this, tourism corporations turn to strengthening their basis by means of widening the assortment of cheaper, mass products. Thus they knock the competitors out from the outskirts of their "profit zone".

Many hotel chains are using this model in their business operations, especially those in the category of 4-5*. For example, the Cendant corporation was initially managing several brands of luxury hotels. However, when facing the emerging competition on the side of motel chains and mid-price hotels, this corporation made up the decision to buy out Day Inn and Park Inn, both providing services in the quality range of 2-3*. In such a way, Cendant has built a pyramid of own offers which covers both high and average levels of service quality (and price accordingly). Thus, the company has guaranteed itself the leading positions at the most profitable "layer" of assortment - 4* and 5* hotels. Now its closest competitors among mid-level and budget class hotels were unable to develop their service quality any further.

The model of profit as a multicomponent system is based on the fact that in business selling one and the same product may have numerous components, each with its own indicators of profitability, and only a few of those would be highly profitable. The inability to use the most profitable components to their very maximum naturally leads to lower profitability of the whole system. On the other hand, less profitable components are also necessary since they guarantee the stable provision of the more profitable ones.

For example, sales of one and the same tourist product may be carried out through a distribution system (online, in the offices of authorized agents, via corporate contracts etc.). And exactly the same product can be also offered via less promising channels of distribution, for example, through independent contract-based tourist agents (cooperation with them always means that the TNC would need to pay a relatively high commission fee and at the same time spend more due to transfer of commercial information and trying to increase loyalty).

Still, corporations do not exclude this option from their list of distribution channels because its presence within this common system of distribution - even though being more expensive - still works for the corporations, supporting its brand and disseminating information on it. And in some specific cases this channel may turn to be more efficient than own, usually more profitable, channels of a tourist product distribution. This may happen, for example, when an independent agent is able to cover a highly specific group of consumers. Yes, in this case the independent agent will, most probably, demand a higher commission fee along with some investments on the side of a transnational tourist operator. On the other hand, if this independent agent is able to offer a large enough database of regular clients, cooperation would turn to be even more efficient than quick online sales.

Transnational tourist companies have all the capacities for parallel development of all system components, including those with the lowest indicators of profitability. This means that large tourist business does not need to restructure every time they need to prioritize a certain, more profitable channel. And this saving on restructuring means there are more resources and time to maintain own leading position at the consumer market, accumulating even more profit.

This strategy has been used by nearly all transnational corporations implementing the expansion strategy in relation to new markets. When entering new markets, TNCs do not build brand new distribution systems. Instead, they buy out the most stable intermediaries working on this new market, turning them into a consolidated network of agents. This means that the parent company does not need to trouble itself with how profitable is each new unit joining the corporate network.

The model of outstripping profit rests on the idea that in tourist business all advantages go to the pioneer of a market. And this pioneer is able to keep their hyper-profit until the followers are able to reach out to the premium. The key profit factor in this model is unique offer. Uniqueness makes all extra charges possible until the moment when the closest competitor comes up with a similar offer.

The key success factor in the model of outstripping profit is not the time of entering the market with a new product, but rather the opportunity (and/or the capacity) to prevent the nearest competitor from doing the same. How to held competitors back for a long enough time so that to get the maximal profit in the several first months from the date of a brand new product introduction to the market? This is what brand is for, and transnational tourism corporations surely have powerful enough brands to make use of the outstripping profit most effectively.

TNCs with the strongest brands are able to present nearly any new product at nearly any regional market at no time. Moreover, if the closest competitor fails to build up a brand with a similar marketing power soon enough - they will also fail to present their new product with the same success. Therefore, the pioneer of the market will still be getting their hyper-profit.

According to the model of multiple profit, tourist corporation would be able to benefit more using one and the same product, its key feature, its classical package of services etc. This model is usually used by businesses that have managed to create consumer brands with high level of recognizability. First the company invests quite a lot, of course, into the creation of its brand. However, at later stages it can license it and use it further on a much wider range of the associated products (not always directly related to its core product).

In the tourism sector hotel chains apply this strategy most frequently. They may establish their own travel companies or even branded resorts (as, for example, ACCOR). Airlines also use this model when they add tourism to the list of their businesses in an attempt to make use of their parent brand (as British Airways). And even financial companies are known to use this model (the most popular example being American Express that is also offering travels these days).

Another popular trend in the tourism sector in this regard is marketing the "merged brands" which are offering a joint product together (in this case the brands are not really merged, in the full meaning). New products to European products, for example, have been offered branded as TUI-Lufthansa or Kuoni-Swiss. Clearly, the more known is a particular brand at the tourist market - the stronger are its market capacities and the wider would be its circle of potentially loyal clients, the more opportunities it will get for multiple income.

On their pathway to commercial success companies inevitably scale up their activities, thus, they also become more formalized and more distanced from their clients. This means that speed of their reaction to consumer demand and changes in it would be getting only slower. In order to overcome all these negative consequences tourist corporations take various organizational measures. For example, they can divide their general structure into several smaller centers of profit generation. This will allow increasing the level of responsibility for the end result, and at the same time this allows keeping a relatively close contact with clients. Thus, we have one more model of stable profit generation for a tourist TNC - the model of the entrepreneurial-type profit.

This model is actively used by the globally known German tourist giant TUI. It intentionally detaches its regional structures, giving them enough freedom and responsibility in setting closer relations with local consumers (and top managers of these structural units take full personal responsibility for the financial indicators of success). Moreover, the parent company may breed artificial competition at the local markets, thus stimulating innovative process inside its own subsidiary and provoking it to demonstrate a strong competitive advantage as compared to local, smaller competitors.

The model of profit based on the initial client database stems from the capacity of a tourist corporation to offer those clients that once came to them all further developed products and services, thus making use from the diversification strategy as well. For example, a tourist company may come up with offering the services of a specific bank or insurance company (which are also structural units of a tourist corporation). In such a way tour operators are able to maintain nearly constant growth of sales volume since their clients will be in any case using the services of airlines, restaurants, hotels, car rentals etc. The more diversified is the package of a tourist TNC - the more additional services it is able to offer to its clients, regular and future ones. Therefore, the more affiliated businesses a corporation has - the larger effect it may get from the initial database of clients.

For any transnational business it is highly important when its branch (representative office) is the largest in its region or is the country leader by a certain parameter (certain tourist destination, for example). If this is so, another model can be applied to reach the zone of stable profit. It can be called the model of profit based on regional leadership. Average consumers of tourist products can be equally loyal to branches of the world known tourist brands or to much smaller enterprises that are leading at the tourist market of a particular region (country). In most cases clients would prefer enterprises with longer history at a particular market and/or the one which is more specialized and adapted to this market. This feature alone is able to guarantee quite stable profits in the long term.

Transnational corporations in tourism are able to affiliate into the own structure those local companies that have reached the status of regional leaders, or they can "breed" their own regional champions, using huge marketing and financial opportunities available only to corporations. Both variants would guarantee TNCs a stable distribution channel along with a circle of loyal local consumers.

One of the most peculiar features of tourist business is its cyclicity, or seasonality. However, large tourist companies have nearly unlimited geography of operations which means they are able to maintain high volume of sales all the year around, thus overcoming seasonal fluctuations in demand for tourist product. Due to much wider geographical choice corporations are also able to have much more flexible price policies and change their set of offers much quicker.

Besides, fluctuations in demand at the consumer market depend mostly on rather unbalanced distribution of free time by consumers of tourist products (plainly speaking, there is always a specific season for vacationing in nearly all countries worldwide). TNCs are able to overcome this problem as well since they may easily redirect the sales to consumer markets in other countries (with different preferences for vacation time).

This feature of transnational tourism business is to some extent similar to another H - hyper-positioning, however, economic efficiency of the former allows considering it specifically within the frameworks of transnational companies' hyper-profits.

Capacities of tourism TNCs to have larger sales' volumes and to get more profit around the year without pauses naturally leads to a tremendous increase in the overall indicators of financial success. This factor excludes unnecessary spending on maintenance during the low season (other companies throughout the whole low seasons are forced to spend much more: on keeping up the employees' motivation, their trainings, on advertisement and promotion, on modernization of equipment and restructuring of processes. Also, some of the partners and suppliers may leave during the low season, so additional funds go on search for the alternative).

Another model of transnational corporations' profit stems from the fact that TNCs always have the larger market share. In any type of business actually companies with a larger market share demonstrate higher profitability and get various price-related advantages and also economy on scale. Partially this happens because these companies are able to accumulate truly priceless production experiences and valuable skills of working with huge volumes of products and services (though this is not the only reason, of course).

Table 4.1. Advantages of tourism TNCs in the field of hyper-profit formation

Model used	Advantages obtained by TNCs
1. Model of profit from consumer decisions	- an opportunity to invest heavily in marketing and consumer market research; - having more time to initiate new types of business activity; - active growth which is taking into account consumer preferences and increasing corporate efficiency at the same time
2. Model of profit based on the product pyramid formation	- vast opportunities to diversify own offer; - opportunity and capacity to merge competitors that are trying to offer a cheaper product/service; - financial capacity to carry out a thorough strategic analysis of the competitive environment
3. Model of profit based on the multicomponent system	- capacity to organize parallel distribution of a corporate product through various channels with very different levels of profitability; - a chance to avoid the restructuring of distribution channels for quite a long time

4. Model of outstripping profit	- extra financial capacities to develop own innovations and present them to the tourist market; - more opportunities for marketing support when a brand new tour is being offered; - strong protection from competitors (who are often also followers); - capacity to create entry barriers or artificially strengthen the already existing ones
5. Model of multiple profit	- owning a brand and/or a trademark with the truly global power; - vast marketing opportunities to support and/or boost the efficient use of this brand/ trademark
6. Model of profit of the entrepreneurial type	- having a flexible organizational structure; - an opportunity to detach certain structural groups and strategic zones of business
7. Model using the initially formed database of clients	- huge database of clients; - there is always an opportunity to offer "old" clients a wider choice of products and services, including those most recently introduced
8. Model based on regional leadership	- capacity to buy out the regional leaders of the tourist market; - sufficient enough financial and marketing capacities to "breed" own regional champions in tourism

9. Model based on the cyclicity of offer and proposition	- differentiating tourist offer and having flexible price policy; - operating at several very different (in terms of demand and preferences) regional consumer markets
10. Model based on a large enough market share	- a chance to get a larger market share in a region; - financial and marketing strengths applied to protect this larger share from regional competitors
11. Model of profit based on lower expenses	- capacity to lower the prime cost of own product by means of business vertical integration; - capacity to lower the prime cost of own product by means of lower transaction costs; - capacity to lower the prime cost of own product using tax planning and transfer pricing.

In such companies advertisement expenses and fixed expenditures are overall lower, while profits from sales are much higher. Transnational tourism companies clearly take use of this advantage at nearly all regional markets, therefore, they are able to enjoy really high rate of profit growth.

Finally, yet another important source of hyper-profit formation for tourist TNCs is already mentioned (and not once) scale effect. This effect means, first and foremost, that the prime cost of a tourist product can be reduced with the growing volumes on the global scale.

To sum up, all of the considered above models applied to move corporations to the zone of stable and high profit prove, yet another time, that transnational corporations today really have colossal advantages in comparison with small and mid-sized businesses operating in the tourism sector. Let's outline all these advantages in a more visual way (see Table 4.1).

New level of competitiveness – hyper-competitiveness

Competitiveness of tourism TNCs stems from their capacity to reach the optimal balance between the price and the quality of the produced tourist product. As it was already mentioned, tourism TNCs are quite able to reach the minimal level of cost for their produce due to scale effect in the production of tourist services. They can also have smart tax planning and make full use of transfer pricing, analyzing the differences in tax regimes of different states and territories engaged in their internal corporate processes.

On the other hand, tourist TNCs also have the opportunity to increase the quality of own product, first of all, through exclusion of independent and not really necessary agents from their production processes. In this case, TNC creates its own intracorporate resources and production factors. At the same time it imposes common standards of servicing and production process organization on all its branches, thus guaranteeing higher quality to consumers and lowering the probability of failures and errors in the process of servicing clients.

In this way tourism TNCs are reaching the level of hyper-competitiveness of its offer, actively using two important instruments at the same time - price optimization and quality increase.

Another reason of tourism TNCs' hyper-competitiveness is their capacity to combine efficiently the most competitive features of not only separate suppliers but of the whole states (or tourist destinations).

In this regard we also need to note that if a country has absolute advantages (natural or acquired in some way) for the production of a national tourist service, then the level of production expenses would be lower than in other countries.

Consequently, if a country has this absolute competitive advantage - it can offer its own tourist product to the world market, importing many other necessary products, including even those of high socioeconomic importance for own development.

Absolute and relative advantages of various countries of the world differ significantly due to a range of objective static reasons (climate, natural conditions, geographical location, proximity to seas, landscapes, historic and cultural potential etc.) and also due to dynamic reasons (state of infrastructure development, visa regime, political situation and stability, level of population welfare etc.). Therefore, it would be logical to assume that any country involved (at least to some extent) in the world tourist service production has either high, or low competitiveness of the national tourism sector.

Scientists and experts have been making numerous attempts to rank countries of the world by the level of their competitiveness at the world tourism market. Some rankings have been based on the statistical indicators of national tourism development (for example, the RCA methodology *(Ushakov, 2006),* others were making use of more subjective assessments (for example, ratings created on the basis of tourists' feedback (Zdorov, 2003) or information provided by tourist agencies *(data from Laboratory of BANCO information system, www. Tourdom.ru).*

Gaps in the competitiveness levels between the countries which are active participants of the international production of tourist services usually have an immediate impact on the general condition and the structure of the international tourism market. More competitive national industries attract much more attention of the international tour operators, and this leads to the reduced variety of offers at the international tourism market overall. Therefore, competitiveness of international corporations operating in the tourism sector is directly correlated with the competitiveness level of the states they are working with.

Transnational corporations are able to avoid this limitation since they are free from this dependence on a particular country and have enough power to shape their own competitiveness, using the most competitive features of the dozens of countries at the same time. TNCs can relatively quickly redistribute their intracorporate financial flows (which are also international, technically speaking), they can make full use of their colossal marketing capacities and their immediate access to consumer markets of the most active (in travel) countries - and thus corporations can come up with a much optimized combination of the competitive advantages from very different tourist destinations.

Any rise or even fall in the competitiveness level of separate countries at the tourist market can be used by a TNC most efficiently so that to increase own corporate advantage. For this, corporations apply the intracorporate instruments of restructuring, shuffling their financial, information, human and technological flows. Where a state fails, and so does the local tour operator - transnational corporation would only benefit.

The third source of hyper-competitiveness for today's tourist TNCs is their obvious technological leadership on the global scale *(Ushakov, 2017c)*. Technology is the key factor of tourist production, and both research and practitioners would surely confirm that.

Also, studies on the foreign direct investment during the 1990s have shown that corporations with higher levels of technological development usually create more branches abroad as compared to less technologically developed companies *(for example, Voorhees et al, 1992; Robins, 2006; Bakan, 2004)*. In contemporary tourism business technologies have become one of the fundamental production factors, allowing corporation compete equally successfully at both internal and external tourism markets.

Transnationalize your brand!
and the effect of "office everywhere"

The third of hyper-features inherent to transnational tourism corporations is their hyper-presence at regional sectoral markets. The major causes for this hyper-presence are the globality of their brand management and the necessity to have direct access to the resources necessary for tourist services' production. Also, communication with end consumers is much more efficient and prospective in case of immediate presence at a market.

Transnational corporations adequately represented through their affiliated structures at all potentially promising tourist markets (of both countries-donors and countries-recipients) are able to create global intrabrand space where end consumers find themselves once they purchase a tour.

The global tourism brand covers the functioning of all tour agents, tour operators, airlines, hotels, excursion firms etc., at nearly every country where the tourist travels. Thus, clients are able to purchase any type of a tourist product and rest assured as to its quality which is covered by the brand (trademark).

Therefore, consumers got the feeling of a "one common office" which employs everyone involved in a tour - from a bus driver responsible for the airport transfer to hotel staff, excursion guides and the tour agent back at home. And this effect is achieved not only through common corporate standards of a TNC, but also by the unity of brand which covers the whole structure of a transnational tourism corporations - from the endpoint of sale to the initial producer of a tourist product.

As it was already mentioned above, a strong brand is created using manifold promotion instruments, including the means of advertisement and PR, for quite a long term. But the most effective method to raise loyalty among consumers is making them return for one more purchase or at least spread a word among potential clients. For the global tourist brands of transnational corporations personal experience of clients becomes a valuable instrument of loyal clients' circle formation.

First of all, transnational companies have high volumes of sales which means they also have huge databases of clients. Each of these clients can be turned into a regular client or at least a "talking client", provided this corporation is able to demonstrate an obvious competitive advantage of its tourist product or if this corporation is aggressively implementing its corporate program of consumer loyalty.

Besides, it is much easier to make loyal the client who is already within the intrabrand global space, rather than find a new one. Noteworthy, disappointment of a client in service quality or in its competitiveness as compared to other products at the market may be often compensated - by higher quality of an additional service, for example. This, in the end, may leave the client with the most positive impression from the tourist product overall.

For example, a client who has bought a tour from the global brand X may be left unsatisfied by the quality of their flight, however, quality of the hotel service at a destination point would leave them very happy. In the end, the overall impression from the tour would be more positive, thus, positive would remain the attitude of this client to brand X in general. And this is the first step to client loyalty.

Consequently, exploitation of the global tourist brand promotes the growth of its client database. If a traditional (national) tour operator offers its clients a tourist product with low competitiveness - it will lose these clients forever, even those that were initially very loyal. But if the tour operator functions under the umbrella of the global brand - it would be able to compensate for the one-time low competitiveness of a tourist product, for example, by means of providing a better hotel or an extra excursion at a destination point.

Finally, global tourist brands allow transnational corporations use those marketing strategies which are essentially inaccessible for small and mid-sized enterprises. For example, a TNC may boost own diversification by means of creating (or buying out) an external, previously independent, brand operating on the radically different principles and appealing to totally different consumer groups. This would allow widen the overall assortment of corporate offers, adding radically different ones - in terms of price and/or quality. And this, interestingly, would cause no damage to differentiation and positioning of all other brands under the same corporate umbrella.

Juggling with various brands (e.g., different hotel chains), a transnational corporation is able to create a semblance of competition between them. This would increase the competitive spirit between all these hotels, and at the same time this would stimulate the not (yet) loyal consumers. As it is well known in marketing, any independent consumer (with no stable, loyal connection to a particular brand) wishes to make the choice on their own, being guided by their individual preferences only. And this artificial competition creates the perfect illusion of an independent selection between the offers at the market.

If a corporation has a global brand, it would be easier for it to enter any regional markets with any new product, thus increasing the share of pioneering tourists. According to textbook marketing in tourism, the share of tourists who are eager to try something new is usually around 13-18%, however, if a global tour operator has a large enough base of truly loyal clients - they would be able to increase this share up to 30 or even 50%! *(Goldsmith, 1992)*.

This would allow the corporation raise the payback and increase the investment attractiveness of any future innovative idea they may come up with.

Since brand today is not just a symbolic add-on to a business but already a rather decisive factor in tourist services' production and competitiveness increase (noteworthy - on the global scale), all brands (including those in the tourism sector) become the most valuable intangible asset of corporations. Also, brands may become the key precondition for mega-deals on mergers and acquisitions. Finally, brand is the most useful instrument when it comes to expansion onto foreign tourist markets.

Any tourist TNC today is essentially a multibranded company. It feeds on consumer preferences, loyalty and the changing peculiarities of consumer demand. Structure and contents of multibranded management is changing depending on the geography of corporate activities: at each regional market a corporation can focus attention on a needed brand. Larger variety of offers is another important feature of multibranded management: for each type of travel the corporation can offer services of the companies working under different brands.

The second and the third sources of hyper-presence of tourism TNCs are closerly related to corporations' capacity to organize a direct entry for itself to nearly any regional consumer market as well as immediate access to nearly any supplier of tourist services *(Micklethwait,2003)*.

Access to national markets along with national distribution channels is of vital importance for the competitiveness of a tourist TNC.

First of all, tourist corporation has an opportunity to attract better targeted groups of consumers (for example: college students, or residents of the Southern states, or top managers of oil companies located in the Middle East and the like). Therefore, a company can try a new product on a specific target group first, thus preparing a platform for its further promotion.

Secondly, markets may have very different strategic importance as per their size and their capacity to help with depreciation of development expenses. For example, the tourist markets of Western Europe are traditionally more attractive for American hotel networks and airlines, and on the opposite.

Thirdly, a market can be called that of strategic importance when it can win in global competition due to its high rate of growth and als because it can offer serious growth prospects.

A regional market can be of strategic importance too, in case it offers access to the major markets of the competing companies. Entering such a market, the transnational corporation get a direct opportunity to influence the structure of competitors' profits and it can relatively easily damage their competitive advantages.

The ability to outstrip competitors or hinder their advance means a company does not only need to be present directly at the markets of strategic importance. The important feature of this presence is access to the most efficient distribution channels.

Technological progress initiated by TNCs in the field of the tourist product sales is based primarily on the processes of automation and informatization, both contributing to the direct access to clients in part of sales and later, in part of feedback collection.

Advanced technologies of today allows serving millions of consumers at the same time, keeping all these sales individual and adjusted enough. Noteworthy, with the growth in the number of clients the standards of servicing will not go down - thus, overall competitiveness level of the corporation remains also high enough. Technological improvement of clients' servicing must become the constantly ongoing process in today's conditions since clients also have direct access to all latest achievements of the technological progress: today any consumer is able to get quick access to full information on all the offers from several competing companies; real time dynamics of changing prices and offers is also accessible online. Thus, the client can easily choose the most interesting offer from all suggested. Moreover, they can provide any sort of online feedback (both positive and negative) in a matter of seconds. Bookings and online payments have also become instant. Thanks to all these high-tech solutions corporations can reap the benefits of the scale effect: with minimal spending they get a huge number of instantly closed deals.

On the other hand, hyper-presence of corporations allows for a more individualized approach, even though corporations have millions of clients. One client that has booked one service from a TNC automatically provides it with all necessary information for the follow-up incentives' program: the company got their contact data, place of residence, email, phone number, date of birth (and maybe also birth dates of the spouse and children), preferred price range etc.

The available today software used for data collection and storage allows determining the most important features of a client profile: the approximate level of income, consumer preferences and requirements, and also the source from which this client got information on the already purchased offer.

This information would be of great value for further marketing planning of a transnational corporation (for example, in: forecasting the demand, planning advertisement measures, formulating the price policy etc.). It would be even more valuable for the maintenance of stable communication with consumers.

As a result, the client gets individual service (left also with the impression that a huge international company with the turnover of billion dollars really remembers and cares about his one-time purchase 200 USD worth which happened three years ago). What gets the corporation from this is yet another incentive to boost its competitive advantage and strengthen its hyper-presence at the world tourism market.

Go transnational: stronger, faster, further

Hyper-positioning of a transnational corporation engaged in tourist services' production is predetermined by its capacity to transform international economic relations into intracorporate ones and in such a way smooth the fluctuations at the world tourist market with its numerous threats and gaps.

As it was already mentioned in the first chapter, imbalances of the international tourist market, its proneness to cyclical fluctuations and also multifactor nature of tourism as such (since it is a complex socioeconomic phenomenon which is subject to direct parallel influences of a huge number of factors, starting with environmental safety and ending with political and military situation) are the key reasons why corporations operating in the tourism sector are doomed to shift to the transnational level of management.

Transnational corporation is able to transform its production processes much easier and without serious negative consequences *(Howe, 2002)*. One of the reasons why it is easier is because transnational production process has a network structure, thus, it is more flexible and dynamic. Timely restructuring of the service proposition is also much easier for a corporation, same applies to changing the number of agents involved in a particular production process (since all of them are conveniently affiliated into the general structure of a corporation).

We can theoretically assume that a traditional tourist enterprise (small or mid-sized) is also able to react timely to unplanned changes in the tourist market environment. However, the size of potential negative consequences from sudden changes is of vital importance here: what may destroy completely small or medium business would be only a minor damage for a transnational corporation.

First of all, since all suppliers are also affiliated to corporation - there is zero risk in cooperating with them. For example, this means that a tour operator affiliated into TNC structure does not necessarily have to prepay in advance the charter flights or rooms in hotels, since the airline is also affiliated to the same corporation. This, in turn, means that this tour operator has more space and freedom for quick reaction to sudden changes at the market. Direct access to financial, production and marketing resources of the whole corporation allows for quick changes in the already planned programs and tours. In other words, availability of vast internal corporate reserves eliminates nearly all risks from tourism operations.

Secondly, negative fluctuations at one regional tourist market (for example, lowering popularity of a certain destination and thus - fall in the volumes of tours' sales) can be compensated by growth at other tourist markets, all being within the scope of the same corporation's activities.

For example, fall in demand for vacations in Croatia among Western Europeans tourist corporations and hotel chains managed to compensate by growing the popularity of this destination among Eastern European countries, including Russia, Ukraine and Baltic countries. In this situation hotels and receiving tour operators were fast enough to restructure their offer to end the summer season with profit, while independent operators, small and mid-sized companies were still waiting for a miracle in the form of charter flights from Italy, Austria, Switzerland and Germany.

Thirdly, under the conditions of constant growth of the international tourist (WTO experts state that it is about 3-4% annually, with no slowing down to be expected in the near future) transnational corporations get an additional opportunity to improve their financial performance all the time: even if one regional market crashed, similar-size growth would be observed at another regional market, thus compensating for losses at the first one.

Another reason for improvement of financial indicators is the so-called "delayed demand" on certain tourist products which to a larger extent predetermines the market strategies of both large and mid-sized tourist enterprises.

Demand for a tourist product is getting more and more individualized, however, this goes in parallel to the growing cost of service. Despite the worldwide universalization of servicing standards and common global trends in the world economic development, tourist product of various countries remains to be unique, especially when it comes to religious tourism, or event tourism, or tourism with education purposes.

As it was already mentioned several times, transnational corporation has strong enough potential and sufficient resources to overcome the negative consequences from fluctuations at the market of tourist services. They also have an opportunity to make use of the delayed demand and of various price mechanisms. The same is hardly applicable to small and mid-sized tourism companies, simply because the latter can't afford to wait for the moment when delayed demand is not delayed anymore.

Therefore, transnational tourism business today is the only stable type of business organization which is nearly fully independent from fluctuations at the regional markets of tourist services. And this fact forms the fundamentals of hyper-positioning.

Hyper-mobility of tourist transnational corporations means, first of all, their capacity to foresee future fluctuations at the tourist services market and react accordingly. The key sources of the tourist TNCs' hyper-mobility are:

- organizational structure of the network type. It allows avoiding unnecessary and costly restructuring. Instead of general restructuring, a corporation can transform its processes of tourist service production by means of reconsidering the number of agents and units affiliated to a particular process along with the connections between them. In short, this can be described as flexible optimization of corporate business processes;

- diversification of production leading to diversification of offers at the tourist market. Both allow compensating for falls at one regional market by growth at another, this may also include the effect of delayed demand for a particular tourist product, inter alia;

- higher efficiency of intracorporate communications which allows redistributing financial and human resources quicker and to the very optimal level;

- finally, the considered above advantages from hyper-positioning allow transnational corporation put pressure on the external factors of the tourist market and thus be more independent in all production activities.

The last but not the least 6H features of transnational tourism corporations is their **hyper-prospects** of activities. Tourist TNCs have nearly endless opportunities for further growth. This applies to their economic power and also to their market share since their presence nearly fully excludes the chance for new competitors to emerge. Consequently, there is very low probability of further restructuring of the world tourism market.

All positive effects and all additional incomes from the overall growth of tourism worldwide (again, by about 4% with every new year to come) is shared only between the largest players of the tourist markets, that is, between transnational corporations. Even if, speaking hypothetically, world tourism will go down and/or popularity of its key destinations would be lost - transnational tourist companies would still be able to apply all instruments of marketing pressure they have at hand to restore the popularity to its previous level (again, speaking hypothetically, they can even make people believe that travels are much more important than spending money on own education or buying a new car).

Already today large tourism businesses are able to "orchestrate" massive tourist flows, and their mass management proves to be much more efficient than the one of national governments and other politicians. Thus, we can state that transnational corporations - once emerged as a counterbalance to market instability - managed to fulfill their initial goal.

Activities of transnational companies contributes to stabilization of the international tourism development. However, this demands corporations took really a lot of efforts on preventing military conflicts or revolutions, criminality rate growth or environmental problems' escalation in the most popular destinations worldwide.

It would also logical to assume that in political and social fields of many states foreign corporations seem to be much more powerful regulators than local governments. Consequently, we may even expect that at some point in the future transnational businesses would merge with national authorities. This is especially relevant for those developing economies where tourism is the only (or the top-priority) source of income. In this case state authorities seem to have very limited choice - either to agree for this sort of "cooperation", or to try resisting the inevitable.

TO SUM UP

It is nearly impossible to forecast what are further prospects and new horizons in the transnational tourist business development. However, we can state with much confidence that global tourism would continue its growth and development in the direction of further consolidation. Already today TNCs have all capacities and opportunities to monopolize the world tourism business, and these capacities are only growing with every new year, partially due to the growth of TNCs' own internal reserves, and partially - due to the trends of ongoing globalization and liberalization.

The considered above hyper-features of transnational tourism corporations are not developing in isolation from each other. They intertwine, moreover, they are often in mutual cause-effect relations which lead to additional synergy and increased economic efficiency of transnational tourism. The latter, already today, can be called the one truly globally competitive type of activity in the services' sector.

Chapter 5

Organization of network basis for transnational tourism activity

ABSTRACT

From the standpoint of the system theory, TNCs are open complex socioeconomic systems functioning under the conditions of constant change and low predictability of the external environment. Traditional managerial approaches to organizational structure which are based on linear, functional or linear-functional models, cannot be simply copied and reapplied in the transnational corporate context. Mostly because TNCs do not have an exact stable structure and usual order of managerial chains based on preset criteria. Borders of transnational corporate organizations are not static, and relations between units inside them differ significantly from traditional vertical and horizontal relations. All relations within corporate environment are two-sided (e.g., manager - project group or manager - team).

This chapter offers the investigation of brand new forms of corporate management organization, taking into account the peculiarities of transnational companies' operations at today's global tourism market.

Managerial divisions and other, less needed, fundamentals of transnationalization

Retrospective analysis of TNCs' activity in the tourism sector allows determining several major approaches to their organizational structures based on divisional management and also creation of alliances and unions (e.g., strategic business zones, centers of responsibility, centers of investment etc.) inside a corporation. Both these models have been actively used by transnational companies in the near past. Determined drawbacks of these models along with the growing necessity to consider the specificity of tourism as a separate type of commercial activity require setting the brand new principles of organizational structures' formation - the so-called adaptive models.

Divisional structure of management dates back to the 1930s, it emerged as a natural consequence of growing scale and diversity of businesses performed by large companies. Another reason for its emergence was the necessity to increase the efficiency of management and coordination between territorial structural units of TNCs.

Divisional structure of transnational corporate management is based on the use of divisions built by the product or territorial principle. This type of structuring is very much autonomous in nature: each division is allowed to have own account of profits and losses along with the full cycle of managerial functions (planning, production organization, internal control, financial management, own HR policy, marketing, distribution etc.). In some sense, each division can be treated as an independent business or a separate firm at its market *(Gurkov, 2006)*.

In the sector of tourism and hospitality divisional structure of TNCs was first implemented relatively late - during 1960s-1980s already. It was applied along with the multibranded strategies (when each segment of consumers was getting their own brand, thus, artificial competition was taking place between tourist and hotel brands belonging to the same corporation). Traditionally, managing one brand was solely the responsibility of one division which had all necessary powers and competences for that.

Further transformation of the division-based organizational structure of tourist TNCs contributed to the widening gap between corporate brand and corporation's material basis (the latter includes hotels, transport, office spaces etc.). And since consumer preferences are highly dynamic in their changes under the multifactor impact of tourism business development, managers of middle and lower levels obtain a much more important role than the top management *(Van et al., 2017)*.

World corporate practice in the field of tourism knows the cases of complete change of brand affiliations (hotels in the first place) within the framework of one common corporate marketing or optimizational policy.

Switch of brands owned by a transnational corporation is an instrument which increases company's flexibility and its operational capacity at the world market. This is one of the reasons why franchising got so much popularity since the early 1990s, in hospitality and tour agencies' subsectors in the first place. This mechanism has helped reducing the costs as opposed to, for example, transiting hotel management to another structural unit of the same corporation.

Within the frameworks of its divisional structure transnational corporation creates groups of subdivisions for better coordination of operational activities of corporation. At the same time, corporate headquarters is able to concentrate more efforts on solving general corporate tasks (selecting the development strategy, portfolio management, strategic planning, relations with key stakeholders and investors, communication with state authorities, standards compliance and control etc.).

Organizational structure of a transnational corporate is based on a smart combination of territorial and product principles. Balance between these two principles has been solved differently at different periods of time. At earlier stages territorial principles was the dominating one (see Figure 5.1), but with the course of time organizational structure has been getting more and more oriented on specificity of particular brands, rather than on territorial affiliation of a particular subdepartment (see Figure 5.2). This sort of transformation can be explained by the following:

- growing universalization of departments' activities in various parts of the world, introduction of common corporate standards in management and quality provision, unification of all business processes and control over them, standardizing requirements to all employees (manager level);

- ongoing globalization of the tourist market which leads to gradual unification of consumer preferences worldwide. Tourists today, no matter what is their country of origin, tend to have very similar expectations when it comes to hotel accommodation and tourist services;

- heterogeneity in geographical presence of certain brands belonging to the same corporation due to specificity of demand at different regional tourist markets;

- wider spread of Western standards in management education. Also, many corporations have their own corporate schools for preparation of top managers for their hotels and tour agencies;

- the necessity to coordinate strategies at various regional markets so that they are in compliance with the general strategy of the brand itself.

Consequently, the process of corporate organizational structures' evolution has led to blurred territorial affiliation of corporate divisions and more active establishment of horizontal connections between geographically distant representative offices affiliated to the same brand product.

Similar transformations have been observed in the segment of tour operating too. Nearly all transnational corporations have chosen the strategy of multicountry tour operating covering several destinations of mass tourism. Thus, the organizational structure of such corporations simply had to follow this trend too. Recognizable by consumers brands were integrated into the very structure of tourist TNCs so that clients could clearly see that these companies are offering vacations at nearly any country on the world map of tourism.

Any department within such a structure manages its business process strictly within the framework set by the related brand or regional market, and also being limited by its own managerial competencies. Thus, it is quite obvious that organization of the divisional structure in management of tourism corporations rest on the classical linear-functional principles. Another specific feature of the divisional management of a corporation is that certain functions and business processes require quite high qualificational level. This is because these functions and processes directly determine the future of corporation (for example, financial accounting and reporting, preparation of human resources, marketing and strategic planning). For this reason, these vital functions belong to separate structural elements, ignoring the usual hierarchy. Results of these functions' performance could be later used by any division of the corporate structure.

As we can see in Figures 5.1 and 5.2, product and territorial divisions within corporate structure coexist with separate other departments - those responsible for corporate planning, HR supply and development, international relations, financial and marketing departments. Clearly, performance of these separate departments is highly important for all other divisions, no matter where they are located and what type of consumers they serve to.

Under such structuring certain business processes will surely intersect. For example, marketing department provides necessary information for strategies' development by two different divisions - the first one is managing Novotel chain, while the second one is managing Sofitel. In both cases the marketing department, while providing this data, takes into account the specific features of both these products/brands. Then it's turn of the department responsible for corporate planning which takes efforts to improve production processes at both these brand groups, while the financial department develops the system of indicators to access these improvements and other achievements in business terms.

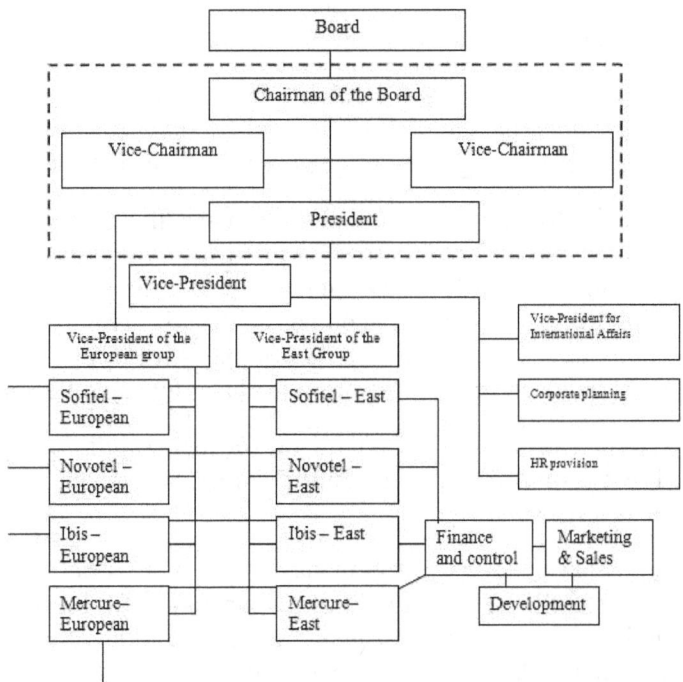

Figure 5.1. Fragment of the organizational structure of the Accor company as of 1983 (made by the author, based on corporate data)

On the one hand, this intersection of business processes within the general corporate structure and presence of the departments with general corporate roles serve as the basis for the corporate construction as such. Together they also serve as some sort of kernel which does not allow departments to be too independent and autonomous in their functioning. On the other hand, with the course of time corporations often change their vision in this regard: on the background of mergers and acquisitions gaining much popularity, ongoing diversification of business and the necessity to search for new incentives (both external and internal) for further growth, directors of territorial and/or brand divisions eventually get more powers (though more responsibility too).

To the advantages of the divisional structure of corporate management belong:

- more opportunities for parallel management of several brands with numerous employees and also more opportunities for convenient management of geographically distant divisions;

- capacity to pay enough attention to a specific brand or product (e.g., particular hotel chain). In this case a huge corporation is able to provide the same amount of attention to a particular product as a smaller company would. This means that corporation is no giant with feet of clay - it can be flexible and quick in reaction and adaptation to changing market conditions;

- growing orientation of TNCs on the end result by means of direct responsibility of divisions' directors for what's going in their offices;

- reduction of levels in top management, more strict division of responsibilities, partial shift of responsibility for income on the middle level of management, decentralization of managerial decision-making, improvement of intracorporate communications;

- more opportunities to attract high-class professional as consultants or for full-time work, especially when it comes to strategically important decision-making (this becomes easier because the core departments are common for the whole corporation).

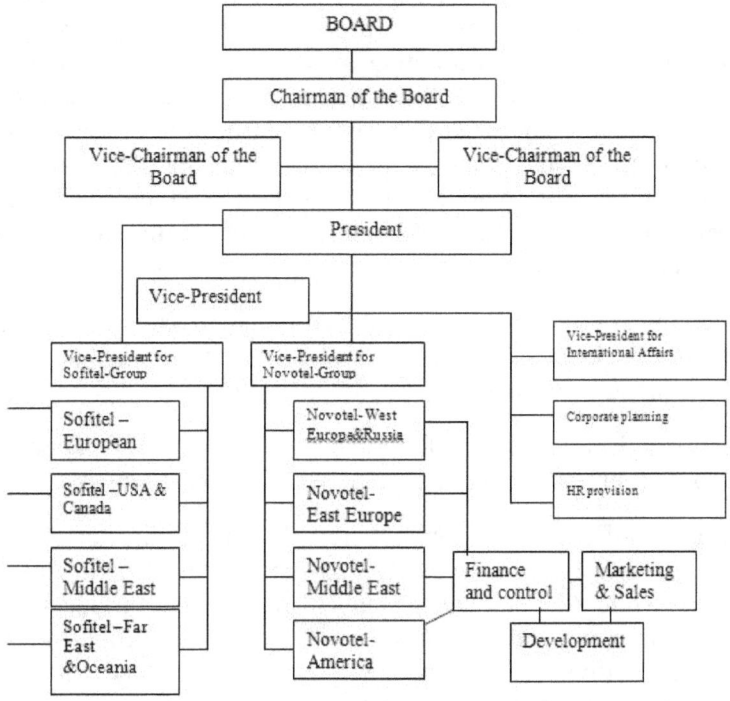

Figure 5.2. Fragment of the organizational structure of the Accor company as of 1991 (made by the author, based on corporate data)

However, divisional structure of TNCs also has its drawbacks and bottlenecks. For example, some of the business processes are merged, while they belong to different divisions and departments. This may cause growth of tensions due to intracorporate competition between divisions. There is nothing worse than such kind of corporate relations since this sort of competition can quite severely damage the unity and the wholeness of a corporation.

Inclusion of the already existing business (for example, as a result of merger) into the divisional structure would require its restructuring due to the necessity to transfer part of functions and processes to the general corporate departments. For example, as in the case of Accor, already mentioned above, all process related to staff preparation, financial issues and accounting, marketing etc. were transferred to central departments. At this, there is no guarantee that processes delegated now to general corporate structures would take into account the specificity of a particular brand or key features of a particular regional market since managers working in this general departments are rather detached from the realia of a particular division.

These and other bottlenecks of the corporate division-based structure became the key cause of their gradual transformation and formation of the brand new basis for intracorporate relations.

First of all, in the end of the 1990s already vertical relations inside corporate structures started to experience serious changes.

Initially, all operational units were reporting to director general. In certain cases he would closely manage also all departments of the core, while operational management of the production and distribution departments was transferred to his deputy. However, even such division of responsibilities and powers was not enough since there were too many operational departments.

Thus, many TNCs chose to have one more, special level of management - groups of vice-presidents, each being responsible for several departments, while all most important decisions were consulted and controlled within a group, the latter also coordinating all activities of the included departments with the rest of a corporation. In our visual example above we can see the key functions of groups' directors within the hotel chain Accor.

Initially, group vice-presidents were viewed as the representatives of the Board and as the key source of information for director general concerning the results of a particular business zone and its development prospects overall. Thus, group vice-presidents were seen not as representatives of separate business directions with their specific interests but as members of corporation's top management, sharing by default the common vision on corporate business and working in the best interests of the corporation as a whole. However, these rather idealistic expectations turned out to be very much unrealistic.

First of all, the very system of centralized investment resources' distribution made group vice-presidents fight for the specific interests of their own divisions only. In the absolute majority of all corporations there are always quite strict rules and limits on capital use according to the levels of management. The overall level of rights on capital investments depended on the size of a particular company, strategic importance of certain divisions in it and (not that seldom) personal features of the departments' and groups' managers. The larger was the volume of accessible for investment capital in a particular division - the more claims the head of that division would have concerning own powers and responsibilities for freer use of these capital investments.

Secondly, borders of group directors' responsibility for the performance of their divisions were not fully clear *(Gurkov, 2006)*. In many corporations this uncertainty about responsibilities has led to a situation when group directors started to take the responsibility for the operational level as well, and very soon this caused mass changes in titles: group directors were now named group presidents, and they also got a new right along with the new name - the right to form own managerial team.

The logic behind these transformations is rather simple. Huge diversified corporations were already quite widespread in the tourism sector, and their structural units were engaged in essentially very different types of activities (different in product features, segments of serviced consumers, types of servicing, distribution channels etc.). At the same time it is nearly impossible to determine where are the borders between the markets and business processes belonging to these numerous divisions. Any new intersection in processes between territorial and/or product divisions has inevitably led to the growth of intracorporate competition (e.g., one division could easily lure consumers from another division). Such inside competition is clearly a threat to corporation's unity and business survival as such.

Under such conditions top management of the diversified tourism corporations was forced to leave some space for potential doubling of managerial functions within the framework of nearly fully autonomous territorial and/or product divisions (autonomous in both strategic decision-making and market behavior). Corporate top management finally admitted that centralization is not working anymore, thus, group directors were granted full presidential authority, including the right to shape the managerial hierarchy within their divisions. Therefore, the divisional structure of TNCs turned into the integration of autonomous departments, under which all business processes were fully independent, while the processes identical in their form and content but belonging to different divisions got the opportunity to develop in parallel to each other independently.

For example, such transformations taking place within the organizational structure of the Accor company have led to the appearance of parallel departments of marketing or distribution as well as parallel financial and R&D departments for each brand of this company. Despite the seeming irrationality (similar processes repeated in parallel are supposed to reduce the overall efficiency of management) such an organizational structure overall increased the position of each structural unit and promoted their further development. Presidents of the groups were forced to find more new internal and external opportunities for optimization of their hotel/agencies' services' production.

Transition from traditional division-based structure of TNCs into an integrated holding of quite independent productions has allowed these huge businesses participate in the processes of mergers and acquisitions more actively. This is one of the reasons why the very end of the 20th century saw the peak in popularity of this type of deals.

Having nearly perfect conditions for business merger, well-established relations between the core and the presidents of the groups, common standards of work and management, common system of performance indicators and nearly absolute isolation of business processes within the related division, TNCs became now able to merge new businesses quicker than ever before, no matter what their size is. At this, there was no need to carry out significant modernization of the already existing structures (merged one and the one performing the merger), and this fact became the key achievement of this new type of corporate structure based on the concept of strategic business zone.

Business zoning as the concept of corporate organizational strategizing

Strategic business zone became the new principle of organizational structuring of tourism TNCs due to growing diversification of offers and also due to the growing necessity to strengthen own presence at the global market. Already in the 1990s corporations working in tourism started to feel the limits of their profitability, and this forced them to participate more actively in various mergers and acquisitions so that to reach more synergy effects and thus strengthen own global presence and growth.

Moreover, the factor of limited growth also forced large businesses try finding new internal opportunities to increase the production efficiency. At that time TNCs spent really a lot of time of their top managers on searching for means and ways to optimize business processes, to adapt better to the market and thus guarantee own future growth.

In the early 1990s, due to all these transformations, nearly all tourism and hotel corporations introduced the concept of strategic business zone. SBZ (strategic business zone) is the department inside a corporation which has its own fixed resources, own competitors and own strategy of market behavior.

The preliminary situation in which a department can form its SBZ normally looks as follows:

- availability of own mission of functioning and own business concept;

- functioning at an open market, that is, supplying a larger share of the produced to clients outside the corporation, not inside it;

- presence of specific competitors.

Transition to the SBZ concept automatically meant the end of the corporate division-based system. In the result of the internal revision it turned out that certain departments or even the whole operational groups were serving only the internal needs of corporations, thus not contributing to better market positioning of the company in general. Besides that, when top management of a corporation made this key decision - to switch to the new principle of organizational structure modelling, based now on strategic business zones, the company was automatically losing its previous basis for all activities. As a result, structural groups became allowed to have their own mission and vision, and also to use freely the resources available to them, to develop own strategy of market behavior, not even taking into account the views from other units within the same corporation.

Therefore, in the course of the 1990s most of tourism TNCs were switching from the division-based hierarchy to being vertically integrated holdings, the latter being essentially the unions of nearly fully independent businesses. According to this model, each strategic business zone (that is, each autonomous part of a corporation engaged in creation of a certain product) was defined quite exactly. At this, business processes of several SBZ were not intersecting though some parallelism and functions' doubling were treated as acceptable. Each business zone had its development strategy, introduced and later adjusted/corrected by the inside management of this SBZ. It also had its own resources (both tangible and intangible), and purposes of these resources' application were treated as the internal affairs of a SBZ. Finally, every zone has its own circle of consumers. Some of strategic business zones inside the same corporations could be in competition with each other, could steal clients from each other and thus strengthen own market position by means of "brotherly" resources.

American tourism & hospitality corporation Starwood Hotels would be a good example in this regard.

This company was managing 20+ brands, all very much known among travellers. The list of these brands included Regis, The Luxury Collection, Sheraton, Four points by Sheraton, Westin, Aloft and some other. One of Starwood Hotels' acquisition was globally known brand Le Meridien.

Hotel brands within the structure of the same corporations are usually managed on the principle of full autonomy and independence from each other. Brand management is headed and supervised by the president who has all the freedom to choose his/her team of other managers along with the full freedom to determine the structure and the hierarchy of management. All interrelationships between SBZ and corporation's top management or between different SBZs inside a corporation have their strict rules and regulations. For example, in the case of Starwood Hotel several mechanisms are applied to maintain the unity of the TNC and prevent its disintegration:

- all business plans of SBZs must be approved by top management. These business plans looks like a contract between Starwood Hotels on the one side and its separate strategic unit on the other (e.g., Sheraton). Under this contract, the headquarters promises to provide means and resources necessary for brand development, while the SBZ managing this brand guarantees that certain level of performance indicators would be achieved. Thus, adherence to this business plan determined the fate of a structural unit (in the worst-case scenario this unit would be sold or restructured). Also, all further career of its president also depends on the performance under this "contract";

- introducing the general corporate Code of Business Conduct. This document clearly describes all procedures related to closing deals, all details related to project preparation and its later assessment as well as many other business procedures, mostly related to the level of managing separate units;

- direct participation of managers in stocks' ownership. This mechanism has got extremely popular in the recent decade especially. At Starwood Hotels over 1,5 thousand managers own a certain amount of stocks;

- establishment of the Board of SBZ presidents to unite all managers of the top level (noteworthy, this is NOT a corporate board, this institution functions separately). There might be also other functional collegiate bodies, for example, separately for financial managers, marketing ones, HR offices' heads etc. Introducing all these additional units into the structure of Starwood Hotels and also providing them with enough authority in the field of general corporate strategies' development proved to be helpful in prevention of disintegrational movements;

- annual overview of achievements and problems in the fields of general development and human resources' preparation;

- internal selection of candidates on high-level positions inside departments; practicing rotation of mid- and high-level management between SBZs;

- carrying out general corporate monitoring of consumer satisfaction separately for each product of each SBZ. Tight corporate control (including financial one) over the activities of each strategic business zone;

- - the common system of preferences and pensions for all corporate employees, from all departments and strategic zones.

One of the key advantages from applying the concept of strategic business zones in the organizational structure of a TNC concerns the appearance of additional opportunities for growth, and what is most importantly - all these extra opportunities are intracorporate in their origin. Under the conditions of intracorporate competition SBZs are prone to be more active at the market, increase the quality of their product, be more attentive with clients' loyalty. Moreover, corporation's board often provokes this competitive fight from the inside. For example, a corporation may buy out the key competitor at a particular market and thus relocate the competition to the inside field.

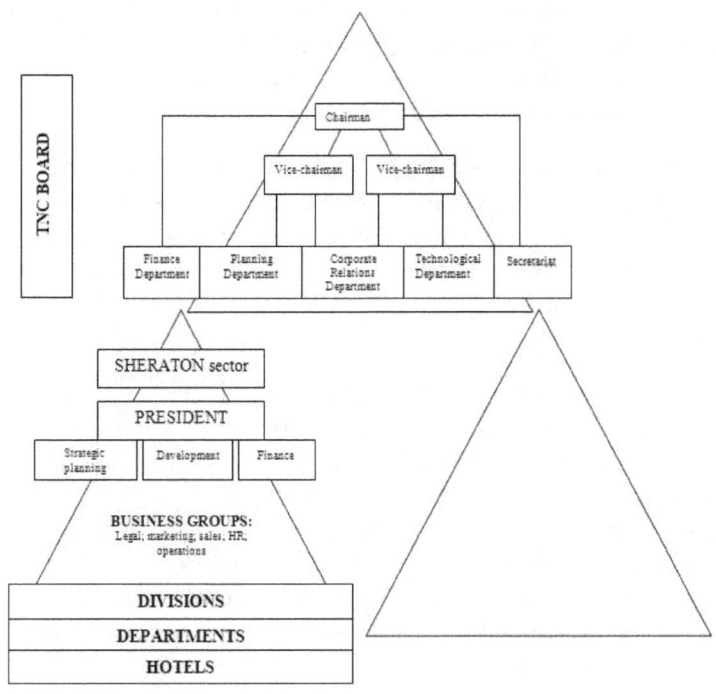

Figure 5.3. Fragment of the organizational structure of Starwood Hotels (made by the author, based on corporate data)

As compared to divisions, strategic business zones are more capable to optimize their internal processes, they are usually more active and more interested in achieving a certain level of performance indicators. This is mostly because they have the freedom in resources' distribution and further use. SBZs are also more innovative and ambitious; they demonstrate more initiative and overall, have a rather high entrepreneurial spirit as opposed to the departments that are in direct dependence from the Board, or as compared to divisions used for corporate structuring previously.

Introduction of strategic business zoning into the organizational structure of tourism or hospitality sectors TNC contributes to business diversification and wider offer since mid-level managers in SBZs are usually more initiative and business-oriented and they also enough powers to introduce changes.

Generally speaking, strategic business zoning stabilizes corporate performance and improves its financial indicators. In simple terms, one sole business, no matter how big and strong, would find it more difficult to survive under the dynamic conditions of today's business, as compared to a large integration of very much independent businesses.

Corporate organizational structure based on strategic zones is more horizontal rather than divisional. Therefore, it is also more flexible and quick in adapting. Absolute majority of strategic tasks are solved on the mid level of management (the so-called presidents of strategic business zones). Since business plan of a zone looks more like a commercial contract between a zone and the Board and also because presidents of zones own stocks of corporations (that is, they participate in ownership), the level of personal responsibility for the quality of results is really high.

Finally, organizational structure based on the principles of strategic zoning is a perfect environment for inclusion of new enterprises purchased through M&A deals. Interestingly, newly purchased businesses can be from radically different sectors, very distanced from the already existing SBZs. For example, the already mentioned Starwood Hotels, if needed, is quite able to purchase (and without any financial troubles or necessity for reorganization) a tour operator, or an airline, or a ferry company (as part of related diversification) or even a steel plant, an automobile concern (non-related diversification).

ADAPTATION AS THE REORGANIZATIONAL STRATEGY OF TNCS IN TOURISM

The concept of adaptive management goes back to the early 1980s when, on the one hand, competition between international companies at the international markets of commodities and services became especially severe. Companies that were planning to win in this competitive fight were expected to demonstrate much higher efficiency, higher quality of products and services, quicker reaction to market changes etc. On the other hand, it soon became quite obvious that traditional hierarchy in management is not able to comply with these changed and much higher requirements *(Mikhailushkin & Shimko, 2005).*

The key features of adaptive structures are the following: absence of bureaucratic regulations in management activities, no clear labor division by types of work, blurred borders between the levels of management and the smaller number of these levels, individual responsibility of each employee for common results. Besides that, adaptive organizational structure may have the following features too:

- the ability to change form relatively quickly and easily as per changing external conditions;

- orientation on speeded-up implementation of complex projects and programs and solving the most complicated issues overall;

- limited timing, that is, adaptive structures are formed on a temporary basis, for solving a particular task and completing a project;

- along with that, temporary authority bodies are also created *(Holstein, 1990).*

The middle levels of management in tourism TNCs have experienced the most radical changes. This is quite explicable due to several reasons: dynamic changes in the external environment of the international tourism market and the objective need to orient all activities of departments and subdepartments on more narrowly divided groups of consumers, growth of competition at the tourism market (including the competitive fight between brands belonging to the same corporation).

Adaptive structure of mid-level management within transnational corporations is based on the following principles:

- team cooperation;

- more value is given to highly qualified specialists, including those who are professionals in their field but do not have competences, skills or knowledge in the fields of operational or strategic management;

- project management;

- maximal client orientation of all business processes;

- autonomous work in teams which excludes bureaucracy and hierarchy.

Overall, adaptive organizational structures are supposed to become more flat - the minimum of bureaucracy and hierarchy and the maximum of opportunities and freedom to use unconventional approaches, creativity and own initiative.

However, absolute deregulation of intracorporate relations is hardly possible since this may eventually lead to organizational collapse as such: the corporation would turn into several teams or project groups that are fully autonomous, with nothing resembling a coordination center.

Adaptive model of organizational structure of the contemporary transnational corporation in the tourism sector is supposed to combine in itself the maximal attention to the production process with care about own employees which includes the creation of the most comfortable conditions for them to demonstrate the initiative and apply their creative skills.

Introducing the adaptive model of organizational structure in a tourism TNC, its top management would need to draw clear lines between various types of activities - managerial, standardized operational and creative, initiative. This is of vital importance for determining the place and the role of an employee performing a certain kind of activities within its general organizational structure. Considering the specificity of tourist services' production in particular, we can outline the major fields where the whole range of creative, managerial and operational works are performed. To such fields belong: virtual, technological, material and intangible fields.

Overlapping of activities' types (creative, managerial and operational) inside a tourist TNC on the fields of corporation's presence shows that the share of creative labor is decreasing, while the shares of managerial and operational labor are growing in parallel to the movement from virtual field to the material one (Figure 5.4).

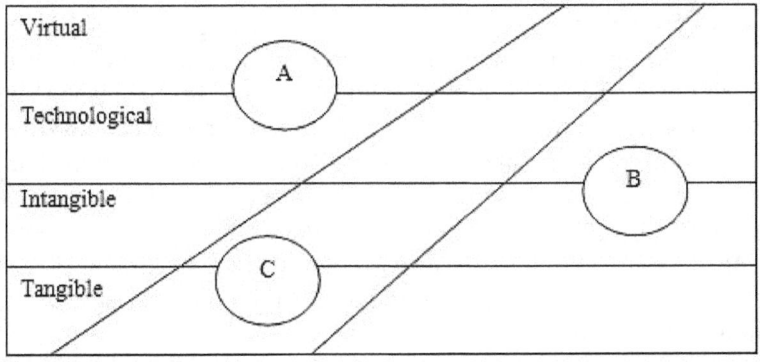

Figure 5.4. Types of labor activities in various fields of tourism TNC

Legend:

A - the zone of creative, initiative activity;

B - the zone of operational activities;

C - the zone of managerial activities.

Looking at Figure 5.4, we can make a conclusion that creative and initiative groups (teams) are mostly busy with the problems of virtual presence and technological development of an organization. Their inclusion at the level of intangible assets' management is of vital importance, while on the level of material assets the larger share of responsibility and actions is the responsibility of operational-level employees.

This division is quite adequate considering the peculiarities of today's tourist services' production and current state of demand at the tourism market. The larger share of tourist product consumers these days are citizens of economically stable countries (EU, USA, Canada, Japan, China), thus, most of them have rather postmaterialist values, the central of them being individual servicing and having an individual approach to every consumer.

Tourism corporations today are supposed to develop own new methods and technologies of individualized servicing all the time. Flows of international tourists are only growing, and the absolute majority of these tourists have their own access to many virtual technologies. Thus, corporate marketing and brand management have to keep up with this high level of technological awareness among current and potential clients. Consumers are interested in having an individual approach in the process of destination choice, they want to feel real care about their choice and to see that a tourism company takes individuality into account while designing a personal tourist product - and a contemporary tourism TNC is supposed to guarantee all of these.

Interestingly, the other side of tourist production, which is consumption of a tourism product (with its maximum proximity to the material base of tourism overall) is nearly fully regulated by standardization and unification of consumer preferences due to the influence of globalization on tourism business and economies worldwide as a whole.

Organization of client servicing is the most standardized part of corporate activities, it does not require active application of creativity or initiative. At the same time, corporate performance in the technological and virtual sectors requires the inclusion of teams capable of creative thinking so that to outstrip the development of competitors by means of own development of technologies and their consequent application in real business practice.

Taking into consideration that every department of a corporation has all three types of activities, we can assume that the model of an adaptive organizational structure for transnational corporation may look like the one in Figure 5.5 (let's call it X model). In this X model of organizational structure the upper inverted pyramid is responsible for a larger share of creative and initiative activities, here belong the most active project teams and project groups of a corporation (A). This model does not assume that project teams/groups are supposed to fit into some sort of rigid hierarchy. These categories of employees do not have direct supervision or any other administrative impact imposed on them. Most comfortable conditions are provided so that these teams/groups would perform the entrusted to them mission and come up with the solutions of both internal and external problems the corporation is facing.

Interaction between these teams is not strictly regulated, same as their composition. The latter should be flexible enough to respond to changes in the course of solving a particular problem. On the other hand, the result achieved is the key task of such teams since it serves as the guidance on further actions for managers at level B (in Figure 5.5).

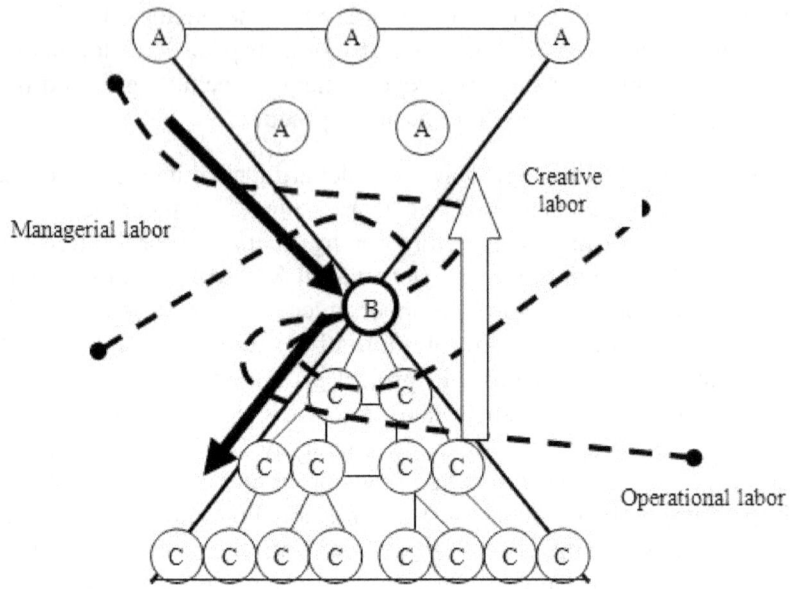

Figure 5.5. The X model of organizational structure for a department inside TNC

Legend:

A - project teams and project groups,

B - managers,

C - operational level specialists

Mid-level managers stay in close contact with all needed for them project teams and groups, and the upper hand would always have the latter, especially when it comes to strategizing. And the managers of mid level, in their turn, are responsible for further development of algorithms and procedures to implement the developed strategy in real business practice.

Department manager is the immediate supervisor in relation to operational level specialists (C): he/she plans and organizes their work by means of creating an organizational structure adapted as per particular task and the managerial decision delivered from the higher level. The same department manager is also responsible for developing the system of motivation and incentives as well as control supervision.

Finally, operational level specialists within our X model are traditionally responsible for efficient (timely and in full volume) performance of all posed assignments as per their competences and authority. With each other, these operational level specialists can be in both vertical and horizontal type of relations.

As it was already noted above, pyramid of operational specialists and that of project teams cooperate with each other (sometimes excluding managers from this cooperation). Occasionally, mutual rotation of staff between these pyramids may take place. Interestingly, promotion of an operational specialist to the upper level for further inclusion in a project may happen without direct participation of the related manager (white arrow in Figure 5.5), while moving a project team member back to the operational level nearly always involves participation of a manager (black arrows in the same Figure 5.5). Manager can easily return the "freed" member of team to his/her previous position of the operational specialist or can offer an alternative position but also within the organizational structure of the lower pyramid, taking into account the qualifications of this employee and the current strategic/tactical level necessities.

The suggested here X model of the adaptive organizational structure for a corporate department does the following:

- it makes sure project teams and project groups are included into the overall structure of management. Under any of the previously applied models this integration would have had very low efficiency (due to inability of teams to influence the decision of managers and also due to very different attitude to responsibility of consultants and experts);

- it draws the line between three types of activities in any department - operational, managerial and creative. Moreover, it determines how they interact and prioritize in relation to each other;

- it guarantees that the organizational structure overall is headed by high-class professionals in the related field, which are members of project teams and project groups, however, it also makes sure managers have strong decisive powers;

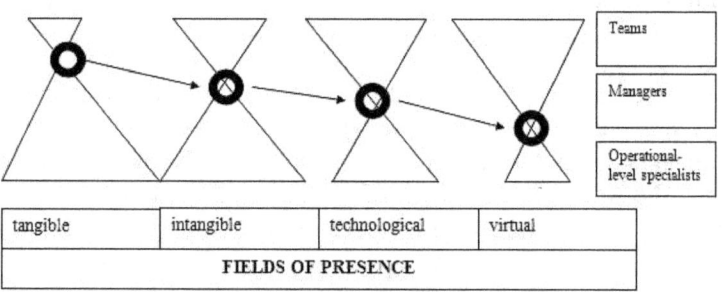

Figure 5.6. Transformation of the X model of organizational structure due to changes in department's presence

- it provides extra opportunities for career promotion and staff rotation (both can be upon manager's decision just as with traditional career growth and also by the decision of a certain project team). In such a way, operational level specialist get more chances for own development, while his/her department gets the much needed flexibility along with the capacity to quickly mobilize the best human resources in case if a serious problem emerges;

- it reduces the number of levels between top management and workers of the operational level (due to the opportunity to interact directly and also due to use of mutual rotation between the operational level on the one side and project teams/groups on the other). In such a way, this type of structure becomes much flatter as compared to traditional hierarchical structures.

Figure 5.5 shows the proportional organizational structure, in it the size of two pyramids is more or less the same. In real business practice though the actual size of these pyramids (and thus, also the number of the employeed in each of them) are different. It would be quite logical to assume that in the virtual and technological fields of corporate activities the number of project teams' members (the upper inverted pyramid) outweighs the number of other employees, while in the material field of corporate activities the situation is exactly the opposite.

As we have shown it in Figure 5.6, organizational structure, its shape and contents would be changing when changes take place in corporation's presence in a particular field (it is mostly material vs. virtual in our case with global tourism).

Black arrows in Figure 5.6 show how managerial unit is gradually moving down to the basis of organizational structure. This is yet another proof that the department functioning primarily in the virtual field of TNC activities would be much flatter and flexible due to minimization of the operational specialists' number (and thus - due to less levels in management of the lower pyramid in our model). On the other hand, the department present mostly in the material field of activities would become more rigid in its hierarchy, more upward. Also, it would be much more regulated in all of its activities, the latter, in their turn, being strictly compliant with all standards.

TRANSNATIONAL DYNAMICS
OF CORPORATE NETWORKS

After we have considered the X model of adaptive organizational structure for a department as a unit within transnational corporation, it would be logical to determine also the model of interaction for all such units functions within the same transnational corporation as a joint open socioeconomic system.

As it was already determined above, general corporate strategy of development, uniting all structural units of a TNC, belongs to the responsibilities of top managers which in this X model take the central seat. Manager (or several of them) are supposed to concentrate all their efforts on the interaction of creative staff and operational level professionals. Managers also represent the interests of the related department in its interaction with other structural units and the core of a TNC. In other words, managers are responsible for maintaining the unity of a corporation in the course of full-swing interaction between various structural units with each other and with the core. Thus, managers serve as the guarantee for company's wholeness, for successful implementation of its general strategy, for protection of all stakeholders' rights etc.

Generally speaking, organizational structure of any tourism corporation has come its long way from a traditional, rather simplified geometry to a complex, highly sophisticated network *(Taylor, 2013)*, in which managers stand at the crossroads of all connections. Therefore, we can state that today network structure of transnational corporation and networking principles in production processes' organization become the only efficient method of management which would be compliant to the requirements of the global market. In the first place, network structure is helpful because it can reduce the number of levels in the management structure and it can also increase the flexibility of a corporation.

Among quite many preconditions which provoked the speedy development of network structures among tourism TNCs we need to mention the following:

- high dynamics of environmental changes and the necessity for quicker adaptation of companies to these changing conditions. Top management of today's tourism TNCs does not have the right to range departments as more or less important - thus, it does not provide immediate access to the middle level of management to coordinate them too. The rate of changes is too high, and all transnational corporations have to adapt to these quicker changes. This automatically means they can coordinate only at the highest level of management. Moreover, dynamic nature of the external environment factors leads to the same dynamism in priorities and importance of corporate activities carried out by various structural units (division/business zones).

This means that a certain business zone which used to be secondary and/or not really relevant always has a chance to get much higher incomes so that to become the "champion" of a corporation (who is supposed actually to provide corporation's leapfrogging development).

Since under current conditions it would be useless to range structural units, it is quite obvious that they can be "ranged" more or less equally, however, taking into account the following positions:

- constant complication of both production and commercial activities, leading in its turn to complication of internal business processes and interactions. As the experience of many tourism corporations shows, launching and maintaining stable interaction between the departments as well as fixing business processes to certain regulations and competences seem to be inefficient. All interactions between structural units of a corporation must be open and free, each structural units should have direct access (or the opportunity to have it) to all communication channel inside the company. Moreover, every structural unit should have the right and the capacity to initiate new channel, and if needed - this newer channel can be internal or external, with the immediate environment;

- constant expansion of company's presence at the global tourism market. Contemporary tourism TNC should have all opportunities to expand its presence up to the limits of the market itself, including those opportunities related to buying out other forms of businesses (hotel chains, tour operators, agencies' network etc.). Merging new forms of businesses, including those not involved directly in tourism services' production (the so-called non-related diversification) would be possible only in the case when the TNC has network structure. Network is able to "connect" the newly merged enterprises and organize their productive interaction with other businesses quicker than any other form of structuring. And noteworthy, this will not require large-scale and costly restructuring or other form of optimization;

- growing autonomy in production activities of corporate structural units. This is one of the ways to increase company's competitiveness overall. As it has been already proved above, granting more autonomy to departments and strategic business zones inside a corporation (up to the level of independent development of their own business plans, determination of own mission, managing independently own resources etc.) only increases the efficiency of activities overall. And thus, it also increases product competitiveness at both local and global markets. Absolute independence inside a corporation is not possible, of course, however, network structure itself promotes autonomy of all structural units, allowing them not only participate actively in the already existing corporate network but also create new networks (for example, the network of own loyal clients or the network of the affiliated tourist agents);

- rapid development of computer technologies and global communications. Technological changes, those in telecommunications first of all, have allowed contemporary corporations, on the one hand, to "lose grip" in managing departments, thus letting structural units float freely. On the other hand, progress in communications has also allowed maintain strict (and often invisible) control over all activities inside structural units or between them. Intracorporate computer network is often the exact copy of general organizational network. This allows the corporate Board not to wait for a certain reporting period but simply check any activity of any structural unit, any time and from any location. Moreover, such monitoring can track down all activities to the level of a particular manager. These forms of control allow keeping all employees on a short leash, even if these employees are working on the opposite side of the planet, thousand miles away from the headquarters. This is also yet another reason why middle level of management and monitoring become not that necessary;

- finally, traditional horizontal and vertical interactions inside TNCs have been seriously transformed in the recent decade. The already classical relations "boss - subordinates" are being substituted by the relations of two (or more) co-owners of business, with a different set of authority and capacities (this is especially applicable for the case when manager and Board member are both shareholders of their enterprise). In this situation the employment contract of a manager can be understood as a standard purchase contract, under which professional knowledge of one person is being sold to others. Classical organizational structure used to be based on horizontal relations which in their turn were based on information exchange procedures, consulting and best practices' exchange. These forms of relations inside companies are being pushed out today by strategic partnerships, alliances and various other forms of unions.

Therefore, today vertical relations inside a tourism TNC are turning into the interaction of two co-owners, both being financially interested in the success and further development of their common business since both depend on the business outcome of the chosen strategy implementation. At the same time, horizontal interactions between corporate departments are becoming similar to the relations between separate independent enterprises, they may have legal contracts signed with each other.

Terminal units of contemporary TNCs become some sort of ports open for inclusion of new elements into the corporate network through the mechanisms of transnational alliances of various levels *(Mikhailushkin & Shimko, 2005)*. For example, a network may unite suppliers of tourist services (hotels, airlines etc.) with tour operators so that to implement a certain tourist project (popularization of a new destination, entering new market or widening own share at the older one etc.). Once this project is over - its participants become disengaged so that to become elements of a new chain, for a new business project. Since all functions in this case are performed on the contractual basis, any participant involved in a deal can be easily substituted, if necessary. In the long term, this also leads to lower total costs of the network structure in general.

With an eye on changes in the external environment, corporation's board forms certain value chains which include nodes to coordinate all activities for higher efficiency of projects' implementation. Priority rate of a certain project predetermines the volume of investments carried out by the Board into the terminal units of a corporate network. Value chains are highly dynamic in nature, they are easily created, and can be same easily liquidated.

Terminal units of a network inside the organizational structure of tourism TNC are interested in own independence and autonomy in actions. On the other hand, they are no less interested to be included and actively engaged in value chains formed by the corporate Board, since every new value chain is also an object of active and heavy investments from the Board. For this reason, terminal units try to look radically different on the background of all other network structure. They actively demonstrate their capacities and competences, they eagerly share knowledge, they are always ready to cooperate with other terminal units so that to increase the efficiency of business processes etc.

Network structures today rely more not on the administrative but rather on the market forms of resources' flows' management. The logic behind networking as an organizational structure for a TNC is that it forms its own, internal market and even the whole own market economy inside the company. The specific feature of such a market economy is that relations are being set not between fully independent from each other economic agents but between departments of the same corporation (though they also have quite high level of autonomy).

This may sound strange but creating a network tourist TNC tries to localize market relations with the aim to resist the negative impacts from the external environment. On the one hand, network structuring allows TNCs participate more actively in all global trends, making the most of all advantages and chances for profit growth that the globalization offers. On the other hand, it demarcates inside-the-network relations from the rest of the world, thus contributing to corporation's stability while it reacts to various external manifestations.

The effect of localization created by the network structure, allows corporation reduce all business risks significantly and also guarantees the inclusion of the most trusted partners into the network. All interactions between the structural units of a network corporation are limited by the corporate "inside world", with its internal market protected from damaging actions of the outside participants. It is not that important which terminal unit is interacting with which structural department within the frameworks of a value chain formed by the Board. It is much more important that all partners are equal participants of the internal corporate market, any of them can be easily controlled and sanctioned if needed, while strictness and totality of these corporate reactions would be much stronger than that of national authorities.

Localization as a consequence from introduction of network organizational structure allow corporations protect themselves from various political and economic attacks of national states. Network-based unions can easily impose pressure on national authorities, lobby own interests in governments, for example (and in the first place), in the issues concerning taxation and export-import operations. Network organizational structures provide all their members with a range of useful instruments which are used to neutralize the effects from state economic regulation.

Apart from the already mentioned above advantages from markets' localization granted by network organizational structure of contemporary tourist TNCs, we need to mention also the potential advantages stemming from segmentation and monopolization of markets.

One of the barriers for entering the sector (and leaving it) is limitation on participation in local networks. For example, if a tourism company or a hotel fails to get included into the network of sectoral TNC - this may lower its competitiveness significantly and may even make its further presence at a certain market impossible as such. On the other hand, inclusion in a network structure becomes the recipe for success, though it also leads to some sort of competitive selection between market subjects since in order to be welcomed in a network all companies are supposed to comply to a range of certain criteria introduced by the Board. Such selection is traditionally used by transnational tourist corporations when they are entering new markets or when they are trying to optimize their internal business processes.

Fragmentation of one common market space is caused by the network structure of relations inside a corporation and it has one more highly important dimension: lack of common legal spaces and thus, deficit of legal rights as such *(Oleynik, 2002)*. Network-based TNC has its own rights and rules, and for all participants of these network relations intragroup norms are more meaningful than those imposed from the outside.

Contemporary tourism TNC can be thus presented as an open network in which terminal units are represented by departments and strategic business zones while the overall framework is constructed on the basis of X model. Location of terminal units cannot be exactly specified and regulated (as it is in hierarchical organizational structure) due to the fact that their interactions between each other and also with the Board is in the first place determined by the contents and the meanings inside value chains of the projects introduced and implemented by top management. This dynamic character of all organizational interactions inside a corporation is caused by the necessity to boost flexibility under the constantly changing conditions at the tourism market, and project approach to all interactions thus becomes integral part of all daily practices. Another reason why dynamic flexibility is so needed is because inside a corporate network there are numerous departments, subdepartments and project groups that are performing the same type of works on a regular basis.

The latter goes against the traditional principle of labor distribution and also prevents the formation of stable production-related interactions in transnational tourism business. For example, a tourist TNC may own several airlines, several hotel chains and a wide network of agencies. All these hotels, or all smaller tour agencies perform essentially the same functions, moreover, often they are competing with each other.

When the Board is planning to launch another promising project (thus - creating a new value chain as well), it may add to this chain (or exclude from it) any network component as it deems fit, provided performance indicators of a particular structural unit match the requirements set to potential participants of this newer project.

Presence of several similar departments within the general network structure is very convenient in this context since there is always a possibility to substitute one department with another. This is yet another contribution to flexibility and adaptive features of a corporation. Availability of choice also means the Board always has alternative variants at the table when considering new strategic projects and new value chains. This also gives the Board enough space for production restructuring and optimization (for example, reorganization of departments, sale or closure of those terminal units which cannot be used anymore in any of the available value chains).

At this, unity of a transnational corporate network is maintained due to the following:

- each structural group or strategic business zone has its own top managers which together form the human frame of a company. It is these managers that maintain formation and functioning of a network structure. In geometrical terms, structural units are the dots connected with each other via intracorporate interactions which are the edges of this structure. Well-tuned horizontal and vertical connections are regulated by the intracorporate contracts and strategic partnerships, both serving to provide stability of a corporate network. Using skills and competences of top managers, the Board implements the general strategy, adding the needed departments to its general projects;

- corporate code of conduct is closely followed and is equally applicable to all (managers, creative staff, operational-level professionals). A complex system of ethical and professional rules regulates the behavior of all employees and also, indirectly, propagates general corporate values and priorities;

- the key role of the Board is constant development and implementation of general corporate projects along with new value chains. Once a new project along with its value chain are approved, the Board is supposed to decide which departments and units to include into this project. Depending on the importance of a project for corporation as a whole, the Board would also decide on the form and the frequency of reporting along with the system of indicators to be used by managers of structural units. In other words, the Board decides on the "length of the leash" for each division and each strategic business zone;

- TNC has all the instruments to increase/decrease entry/exit barriers in its corporate network as per particular participants;

- transparency of intracorporate relations and external interactions.

Therefore, the model of corporate network structure has the following key features: minimal number of levels in management; dynamic internal interactions; non-regulated horizontal interactions; wide spread of strategic partnerships and contractual relations on horizontal levels of interactions inside a network; absence of fixed labor distribution inside a corporation; network structure serving as some sort of frame in which managers are the elements uniting departments and strategic business zones; overall openness of corporate network.

Transnational corporations operating in tourism are not that different from various other corporations in their today's network structure. They also implement the networking approach, even outside the frameworks of own company, in relation to external environment as well. For example, they have network-like interaction with independent intermediaries, consumers of tourism product and even with state authorities.

Let's take independent intermediaries, for example. They organize the distribution of tourist product of a TNC and they are predominantly small and mid-sized businesses since larger intermediaries (e.g., agent networks or popular Internet portals) would be of interest for a TNC too but not as partners - rather as potential objects for buying out and further integration into the network.

In relation to intermediaries among small and mid-sized business tourist corporations apply their usual networking practices, using the instruments of exclusive or regional representation, and also franchising and retailing schemes. In this case corporations tend to be rather generous in their investments or other forms of support for intermediary structures. Corporations are interested to raise their own agents and later form independent agent networks so that to boost the efficiency of sales and expand global representation. At later stages corporations may return to their usual methods, that is, buying out fully functioning businesses (with their independent brands or those already using their corporate brand, for example, according to a franchising deal).

In the field of interactions with clients tourist TNCs also use networking with all related instruments. For example, they often found some sort of clubs of loyal clients, using their client loyalty programs. This form of interaction with clients help disseminate information about tourist product further, and this dissemination often takes place under the conditions of commission fee for the already active client (the most popular example is referral program, when clients recommend a company to other people, getting a discount or some sort of bonus in exchange).

For a multiproduct and diversified corporation (and most of TNCs in tourism are like this today) it is quite easy to implement all described above activities. They already know how to attract their client and how to make them stay, thus making this client loyal. Smaller tour operator has very little to offer to its regular clients. For example, if a small tour operator offers a hotel discount - most probably, this would be a discount for one hotel only, not a chain of hotels (which would have been a larger choice for a client). Smaller tour operator would not be able to discount on the flights of large airlines either. It can offer a bonus dinner in a restaurant affiliated to a particular hotel - but it cannot offer a supermarket discount or a discount for gas at a local gasoline network. At the same time, a transnational company would be quite able to offer all of these and many other discounts and in such a way to encourage both partners and their clients (the latter being also the clients of this corporation) to purchase more.

Networking with clients is integral part of functioning for any transnational company, including those working in tourism. The circle of their clients includes millions of people in dozens of countries worldwide, and for each individual among these millions the corporation is ready to offer something personal and special so that to boost the intensity of further consumption of services.

And even in their relations with state authorities transnational corporations are still able to use networking. TNCs can "implantate" their corporate interests into the state machinery. However, this would be possible only if a company finds at least one minor gap in the "legal fence" which traditionally stands between the state and the business. For example, there might be a public officer, for some reason, loyal to corporate ideas and values. In the future, this officer might find enough incentives to organize the whole system of lobbying, at all level of state administration, so that the interest of a tourist TNC are duly noted by the state or municipal authorities. Obviously, the higher is the rank of this "personally interested" public officer - the larger would be the gap for potential corporate lobbying and the larger network this public officer would be able to create so that to impose the interests of this corporation.

TO SUM UP

Forming their internal network structure, contemporary TNCs in the tourism sector are actually shaping their own market which automatically becomes an integral part of the global market due to the size of transnational corporations and the scope of their operations. The internal market inside a corporation is always protected from all potential negative influences from the outside (competitors' actions, fluctuations in consumer demand, changes in state regulation etc.). It is protected thanks to all advantages of localization and also due to the capacity of a corporation to intrude in any activity of its "independent" partner.

Once a client has joined the network of a particular corporation - they have two options for further movements: either to increase the intensity of consumption, making use at the same time of various preferences and incentives provided by the corporation in return; or to overcome the exit barriers (for example, if a client wants to change the tour operator, they would need to spend some time on search for information on the alternatives, on the analysis of this information, plus there is always a risk related to such a switch etc.). Clients with dominating economic incentives would always choose the first of these options since this variant is obviously easier and does not require spending additional time and resources on it.

Representatives of local and/or state authorities, cooperating (in some way) with a tourist TNC are also free to leave the network. However, in many cases this would automatically mean leaving the public post as well. And this condition is a serious exist barrier! Finally, representatives of local small and mid-sized businesses which once got access to the resources of a corporate network would never be really free agan. Exit barriers created specifically for them simply destroy all further opportunities for independent economic activity. For example, there might be huge fines for leaving the network or moratorium on all future independent business operations may be specifically mentioned in a contract.

Chapter 6

Transnational players in tourism: regional features of functioning

ABSTRACT

Significant differences in organization of the tourism production process, normative-legal infrastructure of corporate management, development of financial institutions have logically predetermined the coexistences of several types of transnational tourist conglomerates, and in this final chapter of the book we are considering the key specific features of these corporate types.

American, European (German) and Islamic models of tourism conglomerates are described in detail; sources of their global competitiveness are analyzed; factors determining their current development dynamics and their potential for further development in the context of world economy are explained.

Business for all! How is this done in the New World?

The American style of management is most economy-oriented, rich in knowledge, experience and all related skills and methods. It is deeply rooted in historic and cultural traditions formed by several cultures simultaneously. There were two core preconditions for the formation of this model - the constant inflow of immigrants to the American continent and the interactive economic policy of expansion. At this, the American nation, on the one hand, was actively influencing the world integration processes, and on the other

- it was also the subject of such external influence imposed by numerous other national cultures.

American corporate management is essentially based on the individual entrepreneurial initiative. Speaking metaphorically, American business ideology is the happy marriage between individualism and competition.

Individualism, in its turn, is the reflection of such a social construct in which everyone is supposed to take care of themselves. Thus, every American manager has this relevant positioning and a certain role within the managerial system. Both depend not only upon professionalism or his/her competences but also on manager's awareness that he/she is part of local business culture, certain business traditions and also personal experience obtained at both local and international markets.

Once an American corporation sets its tactical goals, it becomes flexible to the very maximum in what concerns distribution and redistribution of all types of resources so that to obtain and increase its income in the shortest term possible. In order to achieve such goals a company would need a rather formalized organizational structure with clear and explicit set of aims and tasks for each of its managers. Under such conditions each of these managers would be strongly encouraged to be initiative, to show entrepreneurial spirit, to develop their leadership skills and to make independent and well grounded decision in the shortest term.

Managerial activity in American tourism companies is based on the principles of individual responsibility and assessment of individual results. It is also oriented on the achievement of primarily short-term, but very much exact (qualitatively and quantitatively) results. The process of decision-making in American companies also belongs to the individual level, just like the responsibility for this decision-making.

The methodology of organizational structures' formation for these tourism conglomerates as well as their managerial process in its full compliance with rules and traditions of the American school of management are also based on the distinct distribution of responsibilities and authority, precise application of detailed job descriptions, formal mechanisms of coordination and control.

Organizational schemes in American conglomerates are built, as a rule, in such a way that certain authority is concentrated on a certain manager who is bearing personal responsibility for this certain type of managerial activity.

Internal normative regime in an American company is developed taking into account the fact that shareholder capital of companies is usually distributed among a large number of investors who are mostly isolated from each other and often require trustworthy information for adequate decision-making regarding their investments. Thus, regulatory mechanisms of corporate control have been historically developing in American companies with the aim to provide investors with detailed and trustworthy information, guaranteeing them (ideally) equal access to this sort of information *(Tretyakov, 2004).*

Developing under the conditions of free market, American tourism conglomerates soon started to differentiate between the function of ownership and the function of control, this division especially concerns the largest companies at the tourism market. Legal division between these two is highly important from both business and social standpoint since investors who are providing their funds and thus owning an enterprise (or part of it) do not really bear any legal responsibility for the activities carried out by this enterprise. Investors hand over all managerial functions to professional managers who are getting paid for performing these functions. Thus, managers become agents (are providing agent services) *(Bandurin, 1999).*

Control over management in tourism companies still belongs to shareholders who are performing it through the mechanisms that are making company's management transparent. Transparency of management is the key guarantee of shareholders' welfare and priority of their interests' satisfaction. Therefore, the most competent managerial body in the American model of corporate management is the Board of directors, while external side of management rests on the well-developed systems of corporate control and managers' incentives. However, we need to mention here that application of these mechanisms does not lead to full transparency of managers' activity and does not guarantee absolute maximization of investors' profit. A standard strategy of a typical American tourism or hotel company is oriented mostly on achieving higher profitability and favorable reaction of the related stock market so that to achieve the level of dividend payments acceptable for shareholders. Since such a strategy is oriented mostly on satisfaction of shareholders' interests, it is always more of a short-term nature and thus does not really go well with the strategy of long-term investing. Also, of secondary importance become the issues of product renovation or production process optimization. In the vast majority of cases shareholders are much more interested to make use of their current position at the market. Thus, they often tend to underinvest and be more interested to speculate at stock exchange. For many American companies this strategy turned out to be truly damaging, leading to quick loss of competitive position at both national and international markets.

As it was already mentioned above, a typical American tourism company belongs to its shareholders. On the other hand, there is a wide range of reasons (significant dispersion of capital, participation of a larger number of shareholders/investors at the same time, formal role of the Board etc.) due to which many shareholders feel more like outsiders, thus, they are more inclined to behave not as true owners of a company but rather as investors who are assessing quality of managerial decisions from the outside, looking mostly at the level of dividend payments and how well the shares are being traded at stock exchange. In this case, well-developed financial market allow all disappointed shareholders sell their shares in a matter of seconds, thus triggering the indirect mechanisms of corporate control (as mergers, acquisitions, buying out etc.). Presence of constant corporate control as such creates certain pressure on all stakeholders and leads to absolute dominance of short-term preferences.

Interestingly, this dominance of short-term priorities has been widely supported by top management of the absolute majority of TNCs operating in the tourism sector. Moreover, short-term priorities were not only supported but also encouraged since all higher-level managers got their bonuses according to annual performance results. Since none of these managers had guarantees they would stay on their positions for more than a year - there was no reason to sacrifice own annual bonus for any of the future goals. This means that managers, just like shareholders, were never interested in investing current profits as long-term investments. The paradox here is that under such circumstances the interests of both owners and managers go against the interests of production development.

Another specific feature of the American type of tourism TNCs is 100% merger of sectoral enterprises (those working in tourism) with the related financial institutions (including foreign ones). This feature predetermines, to a larger extent, the core principles of corporate management as well as methods of competitive fight used and behavior at the global markets overall.

All these features of American tourism conglomerates have also led to popularity of M&A deals at the American market back in the end of the 1990s. Merger deals became widely spread, inter alia, due to dominance of short-term interests of managers, investors and shareholders, and especially because prices for shares of the companies announcing successful strategic mergers used to spike dramatically.

One more feature of American tourism TNCs is professional education of their employees, and what is more importantly - conglomerates are generously investing their funds, time and other resources in this education. If we compare, for example, USA and Japan - in terms of high school education the latter is much more advanced, however, when it comes to university education, the situation is exactly the opposite.

One more specific feature of the American model is unity of standards. American companies somehow managed to spread common standards (lean production, quality control and assessment etc.) all over the world. This standardization is actually quite helpful for tourism companies since it helps cutting costs not limiting the offer of services at the same time.

Using standardization methodology, companies - at the very first stage of standardization - reduce the number of internal tasks to the very minimum. In tourism business, more specifically, the following items are the most frequent objects for standardization: the number and the volume of consumables used to service clients (starting from paper use in the offices of tourist agencies and ending with the number of towels in 5-star hotels); services provided by suppliers (in cases when the latter are not directly affiliated to the structure of the same TNC); labor force qualifications; the very process of service provision, step by step (e.g., standard time for response, dress code of employees, stages and order of service provision etc.).

Evaluating the key achievements from the American style of corporate management in the tourism sector specifically, we need to mention several peculiarities which have predetermined the whole process of transnationalization in this sector.

First of all, we need to mention the emphasized attention of American management to high dividends' provision for their shareholders. This feature has provoked another one - the growing number of mergers and acquisitions in tourism business, mostly because each of such deals got an instant positive response from the stock market. However, one of the preconditions for growing share prices after a merger deal is that corporation, as the key subject in this deal, is supposed to obtain valuable property, and for quite a long period of time this "valuable property" meant exclusively tangible assets (real estate, transportation means, land, shares of other known companies etc.).

For this very reason American tourism conglomerates were prone to engage in mergers with mostly hotel chains in other parts of the world. This became one of the reasons why today American hotel chains are the largest worldwide. They were going for extensive growth mostly, simply following the classical principles of the American model of corporate management.

Universal nature of business education standards as well as standards in production and servicing became the key precondition for active horizontal integration in the American tourism sector. Throughout the whole second half of the 20th century the number of related diversification was prevailing in this regard. Hotel chains were uniting with each other, similar trends were also observed at the markets of passenger air transportation and car rental.

Vertical integration became common for American business relatively recently. By the time this type of integration became popular at the American continent, Europe already had a range of vertically integrated tourism holdings, the structure of which united hotel chain, airlines, tourist agencies' networks etc. At some point, American companies happened to be lagging behind since they did not want to abandon their expansion strategies and were still oriented primarily on creating the added value from the same tourist product.

Still, later on, American hotel chains have been managing dozens of world famous brands, having representatives in nearly all countries of the world, while their airlines have been flying from any point A to any point B. At the same time, American companies were not rushing to finalize the process of transnationalization since the latter eventually meant their finite merger. They were forced to cooperate more only at the very end of the 1990s when competition with their European colleagues became quite intense.

As it was already mentioned, tour operating and retail sector as such was of little interest for American companies for quite a while, mostly due to the absence of large tangible volumes in this sector. Therefore, American tourism business was concentrating on the production of own, standard but still competitive tourist services, later sold to huge numbers of consumers (via agents or directly, it was not that important for companies themselves). Such standardized services were mostly sold via universal tourist stock exchanges that were popular at the end of the 1990s. Roughly at the same time American TNCs realized they had to pay more attention to individual requests of clients who wanted to purchase the whole, readymade package of services. At the same time, a typical client also wanted all their individual requests to be taken into account. Finally, this typical client wanted to minimize the spending of all resources (including not only financial ones but also time and emotional resources) in the course of selecting and purchasing a tourist product.

On the one hand, all these trends were beneficial for American conglomerates, the structure and the system of which were ready to comply with the standardized requests of their current and potential clients. Hotel chains, airlines, car rentals, tour agencies - all of them were ready to provide services to their American clients in strict compliance with quality standards "just like at home". American hotel and transportations conglomerates had well-tuned systems for interaction with intermediaries and using them, were actively developing the retail segment of their service sales.

However, during that period of time American tourism business was not able to produce such packages of tourist services that would be able to satisfy the averaged demand at the market. Moreover, even huge tour operators in the USA were operating under the shadow of global hotel chain and airlines. This situation caused a range of structural changes at the American tourism market at the very end of the 1990s. Large hospitality and transportation businesses started to pay their attention to a relatively new (for that time) phenomenon of e-commerce. Also, more of their attention was paid to small and even family tourist agencies. American TNCs started to launch their own tour operating departments, early activity of which was directed on satisfaction of tourist demand of the clients from their parent company. In such a way hotel chains have been forming specialized production structures which were formulating their tourist package offer on the basis of accommodation in their own hotels. Airlines, in their turn, started to promote their additional services of hotel booking and car rental in the cities most visited by their passengers.

Since this sort of tour operators were founded within the structures of transnational conglomerates, it would be logical to assume that American tour operating was functioning at the transnational level of management since its very early days.

Traditional for American tourism conglomerates is inclusion of financial institutes (banks, investment funds etc.) into their structure.

They guarantee corporate stability and serve as the most stable sources of financing for transnational business activity.

In relation to the American model separately we need to mention the regulating role of the state. Rigid anti-monopoly laws guarantee wider authorities for state bodies in regulation of corporate activities. At the same time, there is hardly any state support provided for the tourism sector. The American state has been not involved in promotion of national tourist product, thus, this function of promotion has been fully transferred onto independent organizations, or corporations had to join forces for campaigning.

Business for the nearest and dearest: Warm greetings from Continental Europe!

German conglomerates emerged at the end of the 19th century as vertically integrated groups. They were quickly expanding and developing in two directions at the same time: downward - from processing industries to mining and agriculture; and also upward - to the markets of end products. The necessity of their rapid development was predetermined by the need for stronger control over spending and quality, and also control over demand. Also, these German conglomerates were performing an important function of social integration balancing between rather high corporate technical qualifications and average level of population education overall. Most of German concerns were family businesses *(Lenskiy, 2001)*. Banks started to play their important role in conglomerates of German model relatively late - only after the World War II.

European model of corporate financing can be characterized by high dependence of companies from banks' capital and very high level of indebtedness in relation to owned capital. Under this scenario banks do not function as competitive credit institutions, instead, they try their best to lure their corporate clients into the system of complex and long-term relations. Capital markets are overall less developed.

As compared to market-oriented American conglomerates, German companies are much less transparent, they choose to disclose their corporate information rather selectively.

In tourism conglomerates of Europe (Germany in particular) control is fully in hands of the so-called insiders *(Tretyakov, 2004)* who are the person with full access, due to their position, to internal information on corporate performance and company's development prospects (in the US insider is any owner of at least 10% of shares, and also any of the directors or other top managers. In Europe or Japan about 70% or more of all shares usually belong to financial groups or other affiliated with a corporation structures. Thus, control over all insider activity is organized by the leading bank. This bank is not only the major shareholder but also the core creditor of a conglomerate). Various corporate structures, shareholder agreements, discriminatory voting and other semilegal practices are widely applied to decrease the participation rate of minor shareholders.

Sometimes the organizational structures of European tourism TNCs (especially those of pyramid type) allow investors with the dominating role in the parent company fully control the branch, even if they have a minor share in it.

Another widely spread way of redistributing control is issuing shares of several types so that to make sure that all insiders own shares with the special voting right *(Pinto & Vincentini, 1998)*.

If in the USA the key owners are mostly institutional investors, in Germany, as a rule, these would be other corporations. Another distinctive feature of the German model is high concentration of shareholder capital. For example, back in 2008 27 out of top-40 largest German conglomerates had at least one owner with more than 10% of all shares. And in the absolute majority of all German conglomerates three owners together cover more than 50% of all corporate shares *(Van et al, 2017)*.

For this very reason owners under the German model, unlike their counterparts under the American one, have all the capacities and personal interest as well to use the owner right and participate directly in control over corporate management.

Specificity of the German model has initially predetermined both strategic priorities and tactical decisions of European tourism companies. As it was already mentioned above, majority of these companies were created in the post-war era already and predominantly within large industrial conglomerates or retail networks. For example, the well-known globally German conglomerate TUI originates from a steel concern, while famous REWE group was founded by the same-name retail network which, at some point, was the largest in Europe and quite influential at the world markets as well.

One more specific feature of European TNCs operating in tourism is the fact that from the very beginning most of them were concentrated on product development. They did not practice down-top strategy and they never started from hotel chains or airlines. For quite a while European hotels and transportation companies were developing independently from the tourism sector. And when first tour operators emerged at the market (German and Spanish ones), they were more like usual big clients with one-time orders, and they were never owners or founders of travel agencies or hotels etc.

In our view, this is the first of principal differences between German and American large businesses operating in the tourism sector. European companies, from the very beginning, were oriented on the formation of standardized tourist product, they were always looking for their own, specific niche at a market and they were also ready to invest heavily in the development and strengthening of their own tourism brands. Quite soon many of these brands became famous not only in the Continental Europe but also in the UK, US and Canada.

Besides that, German tourism conglomerates were developing in the context of intensive non-related diversification carried out by their parent companies, while American tourism business as such rests on the related diversification.

The very history of European tourism TNCs' development is the history of vertically integrated holdings. Tourism conglomerates were expanding upwards and downwards orienting on the value chain of their key tourist product and investing actively in hotels, transport development, agents' network etc. This European strategy of growth, on the one hand, guaranteed the growth of competitiveness at the tourism market thanks to lower prime cost of a tourist product and extra guarantees of its quality (since in this case several intermediaries were excluded from the chain of tourist package formation). On the other hand, this strategy also means rather strict positioning at the market since initially low financial capacities of companies did now allow for intensive, multidirectional investment (for example, in several hotel chains at the same time). And this led to lower assortment of tourist product offers which, in its turn, meant narrow specialization at the market.

Once European tourism companies became solid at their market, increased their investment rating, confirmed their reputation with their corporate bank - they moved to the second stage in their development (in chronological terms, this was late 1980s - early 1990s, at least, for most of these companies).

At this second stage European tourism conglomerates started concentrating resources and efforts exclusively on the formation of their tourist product. The key strategy at that time was getting rid of unprofitable assets or those of secondary importance for the core business. Once they got rid of this "dead load", tourism corporation got another stimuli for competitiveness growth since they also got additional assets for further expansion.

Therefore, at the turn of the century tourism TNCs broke nearly all connections with their once parent companies, since tourism became their not only core but basically the only type of activity. This is yet another difference of the European model from the American one. The latter used to stay within the structural groups of their parent companies since these parent companies were often too famous and too large to abandon them (take, for example, one of the largest American tour operators - American Express - it is still just a structural unit within the largest in the world financial empire).

Another distinctive feature of European tourism business is its marketing strategy which is normally based on the umbrella brand of a parent tour operator. Let's take TUI again: this conglomerate owns hotels under the same name, tourist agencies with the same name, excursion buros, transportation companies and so on. This wide spread of the brand name increases the loyalty of consumers dramatically, despite all possible accusations in the oligopoly at the market.

European tourism TNCs focusing on the development of own brands inevitably led to the upswing of intercorporate deals and projects in the course of which corporations join their financial and marketing capacities.

Intercorporate communications and cooperation in Europe (in the form of traditional partnership and also as mutual capital investments) is much more developed than in the USA. Tourism corporations of the Old World are traditionally more open for joint projects' initiatives and are always ready to enter together new tourist markets or explore together new destinations, implementing joint investment projects etc.

The second important trend at the contemporary European market of tourist services is expansion at foreign markets. European expansion has a range of serious differences from the American one. If US tourism companies are expanding mostly in the transportation and hospitality sectors - European companies are focused mostly on tour operating and tour agencies, that is, on those segments in which they, by default, have significant competitive advantages over their American counterparts.

Expansion of European tour operators is usually based on one and the same scheme. First, the company does thorough research of the market of interests, determining the most commercially successful tour operator at it. Then it buys this operator out. The purchased enterprise keeps its brand (at least for some time), however, at the same time it gradually starts popularizing the brand of the European company. All further moves are quite easy and quick. The purchased company starts quite aggressive dumping, thus forcing nearly all national tour operators become its agents (they simply do not have any alternative under such circumstances). After some time, European corporation would offer franchising schemes to all the survivors at the market, thus increasing own presence at this market to its very maximum.

Under this scheme, expansion was carried out in Eastern Europe, Nordic countries and also some of the post-Soviet countries. Resistance to expansion at all these markets was close to zero since competitive fight again such a strong global competitor would have been possible only in one case - if all national tour operators would have united their efforts and assets. And this scenario was impossible both for Eastern Europe and for the CIS, their markets were too "raw" for that.

Therefore, the key specific feature of European expansion in the tourism sector is monopolization of all relations with consumers directly. This also means maximum presence at the consumer markets. For this very reason today European tourism companies pay much attention to their orientation on client. European companies also became the initiators of global tourism stock exchanges which provide consumers with the opportunity to form their tourist product independently. European companies have also invested heavily in marketing and personal sales, building the whole monobrand empires of agent networks in various countries worldwide.

Unlike it is in the USA, hotel chains in European countries do not enjoy that much popularity, thus, they are unable to play a meaningful role in transnationalization of European tourism business. Until now, more than 80% of all European hotels are independent business units, not members of some chains, neither national, nor global ones. The largest European hotel chains are Accor (France) and Sol Meglia (Spain), they can be actually called global corporations, however, as compared to their American counterparts, their geographical coverage and overall size are much poorer.

Some of European countries also have national hotel chains, for example, IberHotel in Spain or Sokos in Finland. However, in the context of the world tourism market the role of counterbalance to American aggressive expansion is really secondary. However, they usually have another competitive advantage which may be of interest to some tourists: their interior design, services and meals traditionally represent local specificity.

As compared to the USA, in Europe the process of tour operators' formation on the basis of airlines has just started. As it was already mentioned above, on the American continent tour operating started from within hotel chains and airlines (that is, being part of related diversification). However, since in Europe world hotel chains were not that strong, tour operating was developing mostly in the context of non-related diversification of various other parent companies. Today some of European airlines become the initiators of such related diversification and create their own tour operating companies, however, the market share on the continent is really insignificant.

Extra attention to client orientation expressed by European large tourism companies contributes to more positive image, raising the brand value and boosting client loyalty, however, it also leads to the necessity to invest much more actively in intangible assets. If American companies are more interested in quick positive reaction of the stock market and thus prefer deals with significant material backing (mostly real estate, such as hotel or restaurants) - European ones demonstrate much more interest in acquiring foreign tour operators or agent networks, the core assets of which are popular brands and loyal clientele.

At first glance it seems that restructuring of corporate assets in favor of intangible element is a logical trend for today's global business environment. On the other hand, dominance of intangible assets in the structure of corporate ownership increases the vulnerability to market fluctuations.

The last but not the least specific feature of tourism business functioning in Europe is the strongly decisive role of trade unions and of the state.

Professional unions of hospitality and tourism workers as well as of those working in catering and for transportation companies together form a powerful instrument, quite capable to correct and redirect the development of corporate management in the tourism sector. Members of such professional units are actively using their rights to push own agenda in relations with top management of tourist TNCs. This helps maintain the internal balance of the insider model of corporate business used in the majority of European countries till today.

If in the US state authorities have two roles only at the tourism market - the market relations' regulator and the conductor of anti-monopoly policy, the European model of tourism sector management assumes immediate presence of national governments at the tourist market. Moreover, national authorities are not just present - they are active participant of this market. National states at the European market of tourist services are directly involved in the following activities: anti-monopoly regulation; labor rights' protection; international promotion of national tourist products.

All European countries where tourism is (or potentially can be) one of the leading sector within national economy, have well-functioning national tourism organizations, the key goal of which is promoting these countries at the world tourism market. For example, external marketing for Germany as a country attractive for international tourists is organized and carried out by the German Center for Tourism, organization founded by German federal government. In France, apart from the Ministry of Tourism, international tourism promotion is supported by the organization Maison de la France (House of France). In Spain, external marketing of the national tourist product belongs to the responsibilities of the Institute of Tourism, while in Italy the organization responsible for the attraction of foreign tourists into the country is called ENIT - National Administration of Italy for Tourism, and this organization is over 90 years old!

Fraternal business, or Transnationalization of Islamic tourism

One of the core forms of corporate management which has its rightful place in the system of world tourism production is the so-called Islamic model of transnational corporation. Its features are very different from classical Western models of corporate management, however, they have never provoked any resistance in the world business community *(Khairiree & Ushakov, 2016).* .

Today Islamic states are already far from being some sort of secondary participants at the world market of tourist services. They are fully engaged in the processes of tourist flows' generation as well as in the processes of welcoming foreign travellers at home, at their famous resorts and vibrant city centers.

Some of the Islamic states are promising markets in terms of tourist services' sales due to their constantly growing welfare level, their numerous population and often quite relaxed business conditions which are encouraging many overseas businesses, including those directly related to the tourism sector. Good examples in this regard are Kuwait City (capital of the same-name country), Dubai in the United Arab Emirates, Doha in Qatar, Manama in Bahrain or Aqaba in Jordan - these are largest, global-scale projects on creation of free economic zones and also active financial centers.

At the same time, such states as Malaysia, Saudi Arabia, Oman and Turkey are quite interesting markets due to huge population numbers and enormous market capacities. Additionally, the potential of Islamic world to generate tourist flows is partially hidden since many European countries as well as USA, China, India and some of post-Soviet countries have significant share of Muslim population too.

Separately we need to mention the prospects of Islamic states to become the "next big thing" in international tourism anytime soon. They have all necessary preconditions for that: rich history, original and unusual (for representatives of other cultures and religions) culture, high concentration of religious sites on their territory, relatively soft visa and customs regime and also well-developed infrastructure.

Many already implemented (or those in the process of implementation) tourism projects leave similar Western projects far behind - both in terms of size and in terms of costs. Such projects have already become popular tourist destinations for many Western tourists: Iranian island Kish in the Persian Gulf, Dubai in the Emirates, Marsa Alam of Egypt, Port El Kantaoui in Tunisia, both Mediterranean and Aegean costs in Turkey as well as Turkish ski resorts.

All these resorts are yet another proof that governments in Islamic countries are prioritizing tourism development and also have all the capacities to attract foreign tourists and guarantee they will be provided with products and services of the highest quality.

Since the market of international tourism is still developing quite dynamically, it is quite logical that large and specialized companies are still emerging in the Islamic world, and many of them are in the process of transnationalization.

The usual rules of Islamic company's operation are fully applicable to tourist services' production as well. Tourism, actually, is not only allowed by Islam but is considered to be a top-priority activity due to its positive influence on welfare and society overall. Travelling as such is interpreted as having spiritual value, consequently, all spending on travelling and all related activities (including organization of tourism travel and welcoming foreign tourists at home) are encouraged, generally speaking, even though there is also a range of bans and limitations stemming from the Islamic religious tradition.

As applied to corporate management and policies of tourism companies, the following limitations may have a certain influence on corporate rules and performance:

- the ban on any type of activities, directly or indirectly related to production and sale of alcohol. Participation of an Islamic corporation in these types of activity, even abroad and/or when servicing tourists from other religious groups, is unacceptable. As applied to business, this fact often predetermines the choice of objects for foreign investment;

- prioritizing other Islamic states or countries with significant shares of Muslim population in the external strategies of Islamic tourism companies. This prioritizing concerns both investment projects as well as sales strategies' development, expansion on certain markets etc. Numbers say it all: over 70% of all foreign investments in the Islamic world are directed into other Islamic countries *(Zhdanov, 2003)*.

However, this limitation is becoming more and more formal, actually. Internal demand in the Islamic world has its limits, mostly because many Islamic countries are still developing, thus paying capacity of their population is not that high. This forces leaders of the Islamic tourism to take extra efforts so that to attract tourists from other, richer states of both Old and New Worlds.

Saudi Arabia is quite an interesting example in this regard. For decades, this country was notoriously famous due to numerous religious limitations. It used to deny entry to the country for non-Muslims, then this ban was lifted, however, visas were still hard to get. However, since the spring 2016 the new generation of rulers in the country made the decision to ease the procedures for tourist visas so that to attract European tourists to their Red Sea resorts.

Apart from the limitations mentioned above, both internal and external activities of Islamic tourism companies are under the constant influence of the Islamic financial system and Shariah laws and principles of doing business.

In the Islamic banking system the leading role in capital accumulation belongs to the state. Bank investments in the private sector are nearly impossible. This is very different from the traditional (for Europe) system of financial interactions at the tourism market since in the Islamic world only state tourism companies (and of course, they are in the absolute majority at the market) have the ability to attract bank assets for further investment at home and abroad.

Private tourism business is thus forced either to accumulate own funds for further investments in development (borrowing from Western banks is also strictly prohibited), or cooperate with Islamic banks and other financial institutions according to the Shariah laws and rules. This cooperation of Islamic tourism companies with Islamic banks is based on the following concepts: mudarabah - participation in profits, musharakah - participation as partnership, murabahah - contract for further resale, ijara - leasing contract, and istisna (compensation deal).

Of course, these are only a few of options available for financial operations at the Islamic tourism market. In some cases businessmen camouflage non-Islamic financial practices interpreting them in a way so that they look as Shariah-approved. Taxation of financial operations is based on the principle of zakat - obligatory expropriation of income in favor of the poor (in real business practice this usually means fixed sums, in the amount of about 2,5-5%).

Since Islamic economy bans interest rate, neither private companies, nor Islamic banks are allowed to sell or buy money at the market of credit relations. In this situation, companies and banks with sufficient volumes of financial assets thus become comprehensive trade & investment intermediary institutes at the markets of commodities and services. Acting as intermediary market agents, they are able to promote the capital outflow from less commercially efficient segments to more efficient ones. Capital, in this case, is attracted directly into the charter funds of the most successful companies of the sector.

- Many experts are of the opinion that equity finance *(Zhdanov, 2003)* as a method of assets mobilization without direct participation in capital is actually the basis of the Islamic financial system. Others state that equity finance is the future of corporate finance as such *(Zhuravlyov, 2000)*.

- At the same time, operations related to equity finance are not able to cover all the growing necessities of the financial market, especially when it comes to credit funds' availability. Also, there is a problem of limited access to charter capital of companies that are not public (that is, of those companies the share of which are not traded at stock exchange).

Corporate Boards and banks track thoroughly all their financial and investment flows so that to make sure that none of them is directly or indirectly financing activities of the companies engaged (or somehow related) to alcohol production, insurance or pornography. This means that every potential object of investment is passing through the multilevel system of monitoring, with several serious filters.

The first filter sorts out those companies that are producing products and/or get incomes against the Shariah laws. Then companies with high credit indebtedness are sorted out too and also those that are getting income from using interest rates.

It may seem strange first but these and other peculiarities of the Islamic financial system became the key causes for quick transnationalization of Islamic tourism companies, mostly due to the fact that Islamic schemes of financing, apart from mutual commercial benefit for the both sides involved, also mean the alignment of production processes belonging to the interacting market subjects, even if they are located in different countries.

For example, the application of mudarabah requires certain control over the commercial activities of the trusted subject by the principal grantor since the latter is financially interested in success of their new mutual business. If in the European banking system the creditor sets the interest rate and "let the borrower free" for a certain period of time, being interested only in timely return of the sum (credit+interest rate), thus having no connection with the borrower themselves - within the Islamic financial system the situation is exactly the opposite. The creditor starts performing some sort of a patronizing function in relation to business of a borrower, supporting their new initiatives and ongoing projects, thus forming a solid platform for further consolidation of parent and filial businesses. Similar positive consequences in terms of ongoing transnationalization may also have murabaha and istisna. Musharakah initially requires close partner relations between the sides of an investment process. Consequently, if these Shariah-approved schemes of financing are used wisely and efficiently - there will be an additional reason for further merger of production processes of two (or more) initially independent types of businesses.

A tourism company, having all necessary resources for investments and operating at Islamic financial market, in many cases would be interested in opportunities for further cooperation in the same field (tourism) since in it, managers of this company would have enough knowledge and skills to make a grounded decision concerning any of the offered projects.

Considering also the ban on insurance activities and consequently, absence of habitual for the West instruments to reduce the investment risk, it would also logical to assume that transnationalization of the Islamic tourism capital is carried out within the framework of related diversification, when parent TNCs invest in some foreign branches, directly related to their core activity - tourism.

The most frequent and the largest in volume transnational deals in the Arab world usually imply investments carried out by tourist or hotel chains in similar business somewhere abroad (for example, buying out several hotels and acquiring a national tour operator). They also invest in transportation and construction sectors since the latter have direct impact on the state of tourism development at the regional level.

Same as in Europe, tourism businesses of the Islamic world first demonstrated certain lagging behind in their transnationalization rates, as compared to other economic sectors (especially construction, mining, transportation, textiles, wholesale trade etc.). The major cause for this lagging behind was late development of international tourism in Islamic regions in general. First Muslim resorts (those outside former European colonies) appeared on the world map of tourism in the 1980s only, and during the first decade of their existence they were not that much profitable. Moreover, national tourism business of certain Islamic countries (Egypt, Tunisia or Lebanon) was a constant victim of political instability and frequent terror acts. We can even state that in all three mentioned above countries tourism is still at the stage of financial assets accumulation so that to invest later in some project abroad. Also, there might be so that theые countries have already lost their opportunity to develop transnational tourism business of their own due to already well established leadership of Western corporations on their territories.

Due to this lagging behind it also became logical that some of the transnational tourism companies in the Arab world emerged from inside the already existing other corporations, only indirectly related to tourism business. Most successful in transnationalization have been construction and transportation companies, and also some of the hotel chains in the Emirates. Thus, it is quite predictable that in the last 5-7 years all these businesses have come to the idea of creating their own tourism enterprises or tour agents' networks.

For example, the world famous holding Emirates (one of the structural units of which is the most profitable and the most dynamically developing airline in the world - also Emirates) has been an active participant of the state holding Dubai Tour Development Group since 2001. This state holding is carrying out a range of projects aimed at complex development of the tourism infrastructure in the United Arab Emirates. And it is also actively investing in the tourism sectors of Saudi Arabia, Jordan, Egypt, Iran and even some of European countries.

Finally, we need to state that the Shariah-approved types of commercial activities, including those at the financial market, also stimulate the deals in which both sides can be branches of the same corporation, for example, branches located in two different Islamic countries. Such operations tend to reduce all business risks to the very minimum since all investment activity is carried out under murabaha and/or musharakah. This, in turn, optimizes all business processes and all joint activities of corporate structures. Therefore, all Shariah-approved financial operations become the basis for intracorporate relations of Islamic TNCs, especially when it comes to communication between different structural units.

Therefore, we can make a conclusion that the core contents of corporate management at the Islamic tourism market has many differences from the traditional Western corporate management. Moreover, Islamic corporations are, to some extent, in a more beneficial situation as compared with their American or European counterparts thanks to the specificity of their organizational structure, methods and principles of corporate management.

For example, when Western companies come to the idea of partnership and merging their value chains - they usually end up with a flat network-like structure with low level of centralization. Thus, they have to search for new forms of interaction between their headquarters and other structural units. Their structures transforms under the influence of market factors, sometimes such networks lose their best players simply because the latter do not want to change and restructure. At the same time, Islamic corporations by default are all ruled by the same religious principles, and Shariah for them is one and only legal basis. Moreover, as it was already mentioned above, all Shariah-approved forms of financial activities and business partnership as such promote business enlargement and transnationalization in a much stronger way than Western individualism and liberal values are able to.

Regarding international tourism markets and transnationalization in the Islamic world we need to mention several peculiarities which mostly stem from the Shariah-based limitations imposed on businesses.

Since the scale of banned activities is quite large (everything related to alcohol, pork, insurance and also some of the stock exchange operations), most of financial operations in international Islamic tourism are carried out as direct investments. When the act of investment is direct, the Board of an Islamic TNC can rest assured about the "purity" of an investment object, moreover, in this case there is no interest rate involved which is also banned by the Shariah.

When top management of an Islamic TNC, for some reason, needs to avoid the Shariah imposed restrictions, the owners (or the most influential shareholders) tend to entrust the tactical level of operations to Western managers. This is especially relevant for the hotel chains that do not have a strong brand, neither their own trademark (apart from the famous Jumeirah Hotels & Resorts). If they don't have strong brands of their own - they may enjoy the benefits from being managed by world famous Western companies.

Under this scheme of foreign investment the larger share of income is concentrated in the hands of a parent Islamic corporation while the managing Western company gets either some fixed amount, or a percentage from profit.

In this case the Islamic corporation intentionally limits its recognizability at the local market and also sacrifices part of its income flow; however, it also solves several problems related to servicing international clients (including sales of alcohol drinks, cooking meals from pork, providing rooms with cable TV channels, some of which may contain pornography).

Thus, a certain two-level hotel system is being formed. The immediate owners of the hotels are Islamic TNCs, they are also the key investors in their development and infrastructure, they share all investment risks etc. However, direct management, both strategic and operational, becomes the responsibility of Western companies and their managers. Here, the interests of Western and Islamic tourism corporations are not intercepting - they achieve their own aims in parallel. Western companies tend to strengthen their presence at consumer markets worldwide, they concentrate on the marketing aspect and services' provision, while Islamic corporations tend to concentrate on their tangible assets, real estate and infrastructure around, thus, they are more engaged in construction of new hotels and/or acquiring the already functioning ones.

This state of affairs is typical not only for the hospitality subsector, actually. In many fields of production activities or in trade Western companies tend to make use of their technological advantages, marketing skills and more qualified labor overall (especially when it comes to management). In such a way they provide some sort of "envelope" around their capital- and labor-intensive productions. Noteworthy, availability of such an "envelope" usually serves as the guarantee that the produced commodity would reach Western consumer markets, having global competitive advantages of their own.

In the spheres of tour operating and retail trade of tourist products Islamic tourism corporations did not manage to achieve significant results, as compared to Western TNCs. This is related, first of all, to low internal demand for tourist product and also to obvious technological lagging behind (which is especially visible when it comes to marketing and PR, and also strategic management in the service sector). The major consumers of their tourist product at the global markets come from developed democratic states of the West, while their own internal markets of tourist products are unreachable for Islamic corporations, at least as of today.

On the other hand, this does not mean that Arab tourism companies would lose interest in the West, neither this lessens their ambitions to conquer Western markets. For the implementation of this longer-term strategy the governments of some of the Islamic states have already created a solid platform - their strong internal markets protected from Western influence. This is quite promising for these states since their internal tourism potential has only recently started growing, and today its growth rate is already quite high. At this, these internal markets create all necessary preconditions for raising their own, national champions in the tourism sector so that later to "insert" them onto the Western consumer markets.

Of course, Islamic tourism corporations entering Western market is a very distant future scenario, and for the many this scenario may seem unrealistic as such. However, we need to keep in mind that the share of Muslim population in many European countries as well as in the USA, China, Japan, Russia etc. is only growing. And these growing population numbers will soon be able to become one huge platform of loyal clients, when the right time comes to Islamic tourism expansion to the Western markets.

Islamic corporations themselves are very well aware of what is their most perspective product - the Islamic tourist product. Previously, Islamic tourism meant only hajj and umrah (two types of pilgrim journey to Mecca), however, today Islamic tourism corporations are ready to offer a much wider choice of Islamic travels: leisure in Islamic traditions, Islamic resorts, spiritual tours, education tourism (Cairo, Istanbul, Tehran etc.). The growing variety of tourist products offered by Islamic companies is gradually forming a new unique niche at the international tourism market, while the growing numbers of Muslim population worldwide guarantees Islamic tourism companies that very soon they will find their own place in global tourism.

As the final note on Islamic tourism business we need to mention the following feature - the role of the state in Islamic business in general. Many other specific features of Islamic TNCs are deeply rooted in it.

The role of state authorities at the tourism markets of Islamic states is predetermined, in the first place, by the level of tourism production development and also by financial self-sufficiency of tourism companies. This role may range: from the function of control over the quality of tourist services' provided (most frequently this means development of national standards in tourism servicing provision) to guaranteeing security to foreign tourists coming to a country (in some countries this even means the establishment of the so-called tourist police). The state may also regulate prices for tourist services, accommodation, passenger transportation etc.

In the Islamic world the state and large tourism companies are more like partners rather than parties in the process of some sort of vertical interaction. The state not only controls but consolidates larger projects, including international ones, making sure all related financial transactions do not contradict Shariah laws. In their turn, corporations are responsible for creating comfortable conditions for the development of the related small and mid-sized businesses, including those directly affiliated in the structure of TNCs in tourism.

TO SUM UP

Diversity of economic systems, interregional differentiation by the level of economic institutes' development, different traditions of doing business in the countries worldwide have predetermined the existence of a range of economic-legal models of corporations' functioning and management, and among these models we can easily differentiate American, German (European) and Islamic models.

The American model of corporate management, the emergence of which has been provoked primarily by the inflow of migrants to the country and also its interactive economic policy of expansion, is based on the individual entrepreneurial initiative, equation of technological progress with economic success and the system approach to management.

Functioning of the US corporate sector is under the constant influence of financial institutions and their lending funds. The priority role in management belongs not to owners (who are often a combination of many minor shareholders) but to professional top managers.

Unlike their American counterparts, huge production-distribution systems in Europe from the very beginning were forming in very close connection with financial institutions, often with the priority role initially given to the latter. Secondly, European model was being formed and developed in the structure of large businesses not directly related to tourism (industrial enterprises, retail chains, for example).

Domination of common interests over private ones in German corporations means that all short-term interests of shareholders and investors become of secondary importance. This stimulates vertical integration in this sector, including the one aimed at the consumer.

Islamic model of corporate management is based, in the first place, on the bans on interest rates and mandatory social tax. Absence of interest rate and also prohibition of commercial projects' financing by financial institutions together have stimulated the emergence of rather original forms of cooperation between service companies with each other and also with banks. This form of cooperation is based not on strict division of commercial results but rather on the shared responsibility of partners for common implementation of projects. And this becomes the original Islamic platform for transnationalization.

Conclusion

Transnationalization of tourist activities today becomes one of the most important features of the tourism market and a leading direction in transformations of the production process. Also, transnationalization predetermines both quantitative indicators of the world tourist flows and qualitative criteria of the sector's development.

Globalization of tourism has stimulated further rapid development of transnational corporations in this sector, thus gradually turningb TNCs into the only valid form of large business at tourism markets, having all possible global advantages. On the one hand, functioning of transnational corporations in tourism has a lot of common features with TNCs functioning in other sectors, both industries and services. For example, quite similar are the strategies developed and the instruments applied for expansion abroad as well as approaches used in formation of organizational structure of corporations and finally sources of global competitive advantage.

On the other hand though, specificity of tourist services' production, pricing policies used in tourism, competition in this sector and the constantly changing directions of international tourist flows - all make the process of tourist TNCs' development being peculiar and unique. Same unique features gets also the interaction of these TNCs with national governments in both base and recipient countries.

Our retrospective analysis of the process of tourist corporations' emergence and development has allowed us reach several conclusions in this regard:

- transnationalization of tourism business has been provoked by general instability of the market, its proneness to seasonal fluctuations in demand and also overall instability of the external environment. Therefore, initially transnationalization was aimed to smoothing the market gaps and stabilization of the fluctuating international demand in tourist services;

- transnationalization of tourism business started relatively late, in the second half of the 20th century only. The delay from other sectors (industries and even always rather traditional and old-fashioned agriculture) was thus more than 50 years. Among the causes for such a delay we need to mention, first of all, belated (as compared to the commodities' market) formation of the international tourist sector. Tourism as such became global and mass-scale quite late, and at the very beginning of its global journey it used to demonstrate very low investment attractiveness due to extremely high costs of such investment projects and narrow specialization of tourist services;

- transnationalization of international tourism started with the emergence of hotel chains and larger transportation companies. Both had sufficient material and financial capacity for further investment and/or resales;

- for quite a long period of time foreign direct investments in hospitality and transportation were limited, in the first place, by limited opportunities to change the core activity of a newly purchased material object in case the investment project fails. Secondly, FDIs in tourism were limited due to the necessity to develop hotel (or transportation) business in its several directions at the same time if investors wanted to achieve efficiency of a truly transnational level from their activities;

- once international tourism got mass-scale (and this happened in the late 1980s), it became yet another incentive for further transnationalization of hospitality and transportation businesses. Another contributing factor became franchising, popularity of the latter lowered the entry barriers at many foreign markets and also reduced many risks for the investing parties;

- at earlier stages transnationalization of tourist businesses covered only economically developed European countries. Inclusion of, first, USA and then developing countries took place slightly later, once transportation means and communications took a huge step forward. Their rapid development also meant the start of intercontinental tourism;

- today's stage in transnationalization of tourism business witnesses the growing role of tour operators. The latter already have enough financial capacity and also immediate access to vast financial resources of the largest banks. Another important trend of the current stage is growing popularity of mergers and acquisitions in the hospitality subsector and tourism overall. Today, the leading role at the world tourism market belongs to American and European TNCs.

After this brief retrospective of the transnational tourism business development we can outline the key historic forms (generations) of corporations operating in tourism. They have several distinctive features which make them different from each other. These features are, in particular, core production activity, sources for its financing, directions for integration, organizational structure and the role played at the world market.

Activities of the first-generation tourist TNCs were in the first place related to transnationalization of hotel businesses and intensification of transportation. Many hotel and transportation businesses were gradually moving to the transnational level of management, some of them were able to do that independently, without any financial support from the outside, other shifted to the transnational level being part of vertically integrated business structures.

First TNCs in tourism used to have rather limited geographical representation, in which European and American (covering both US and Canada) zones were quite distinct. Expansion on third-country markets was rare and very limited due to concentration of tourist flows on separate regions only, still low capacity of intercontinental tourism and also necessity to invest heavily in new destinations since the latter had hardly any infrastructure for tourism development.

Tourism corporations of the second type (generation) were different from the first generation due to the growing role of tour operating and the related growing numbers of tourist agencies. Rapid development of mass tourism along with widening of geographical borders in tourism became the key two preconditions for this shift from the first to second generation of tourist corporations. While tour operators and tour agents easily found their place in this system due to the lack of easily accessible information on destination countries and the conditions provided in them. Under such conditions tour operators and agents served as both source of information and guarantee of quality.

Stable demand at this market stimulated wider spread or risk schemes in the relations between tour operators and suppliers of tourist services. Thus, in the late 1980s already the previously "invisible" intermediaries (that is, tour operators and agents' networks) became the most valuable customers for the service suppliers. Performance rates of tour operators and agents became the major guarantee of financial stability for transnational hotel and transport enterprises. These changing conditions required from TNCs to have wider agent networks along with recognizable brands. Thus, investments in brand management and network development became much larger than the investments in hotels' construction or transport expansion.

TNCs of the third type are already the corporations with the explicitly leading role of tour operating and agent networks. Previously, large tour operators used to be present at the transnational level of business thanks to hotel and transportation businesses - now they became able for their own, independent transnationalization. Transition to this new form of tourist corporations became possible due to significantly better financial situation of the absolute majority of tourism-related enterprises in general. Moreover, at this stage investors finally started to demonstrate much more active interest in this sector.

Emergence of this new generation of tourist TNC was also closely related to wider distribution of non-related diversification which became the key development strategy for many transnational corporations. Non-related diversification means parent companies started acquiring other types of business, not directly related to the production of tourist services. Many activities of the fourth-generation TNCs were in direct dependence from banks and other financial institutions. At that stage it already became normal that a tourist TNC may have financial firms in its structure. These firms were closely involved in leasing operations, crediting, investing and also in numerous M&A deals.

At the end of the 1990s mergers and acquisitions in the world tourism sector became especially frequent. Conditions of such deals depended first of all on the degree of a particular tourist market consolidation. If a certain market had high degree of consolidation, mergers taking place at it were oriented on the creation of conglomerates with their diversified portfolio of numerous very different types of businesses, including those not related to tourism as such (at least, not obviously). And when a certain market was less consolidated, M&A deals at it were following mostly traditional aims of business expansion.

At that period of time, progress in information technologies became the most significant impact factor, determining further transformation of corporate organizational structures. Due to its several specific features, world tourism became one of the first sectors of economic activity to embrace and adapt all newer achievements in telecommunications, automation, information processing and storage. All of the above prepared the grounds for transition to the fifth generation of tourist TNCs.

Transnational tourist corporations today have the following specific features:

- wide and extremely active presence in the virtual space. This presence helps reaching and maintaining global competitive advantages, including those of hyper-presence and hyper-mobility;

- wider geographical spread of profit centers. This also became possible due to availability of the most advanced technologies used in information collection and storage as well as due to new quality of communication;

- transformation of the whole tourist services' production and sale process into a fully electronic type of commercial activity;

- acquisition of a new function, the one of global tourism stock exchange, which is somewhat detached from the actual production of tourist services, available for immediate mass consumers. This stock exchange provides numerous intermediaries (tourist services brokers and traditional travel agents) with direct access and opportunities for active participation.

The second chapter of this monograph has considered preconditions and driving forces of tourist production transnationalization in the context of several popular theories (interest theory; capital theory; service life cycle theory; and finally eclectic theory). However, we have eventually come to the conclusion that as applied to the phenomenon of transnationalization in tourism sector, the synergy theory would be the most appropriate and universal.

This theory stems from the synergy principle - when joint activity of two or more objects leads to the larger effect than the standard sum of their separate results. Within the frameworks of the classical synergy theory of the market, integration and transnationalization lead to synergy which comes, first of all, as added value of a new participant. This happens because each newly integrated participant is able to use the long list of the already available advantages from integration of businesses.

We can distinguish two key ways in which synergy may be reached in the process of tourism production transnationalization. First of all, this would be synergy effect from the increased economic size of a corporation. This new size and shape provides corporations with extra opportunities to get more attractive offers and better market conditions overall due to their strong capacities, higher volumes of sales and larger share at the consumer market.

The second important direction in the emergence of synergy effect from transnationalization of tourism business is directly related to the emergence of extra opportunities for more efficient application of the already available resources, and not only financial and material ones, but also marketing resources, know-hows, virtual resources etc. The leapfrogging growth in efficiency of resources' use by corporations, in the course of their transition to the transnational level of management, becomes possible not only due to scale effect, centralization and elimination of functions' doubling - but also thanks to more efficient use of capital and information resources, introduction of the most advanced methods in operations and HR management and also diversification of activities and offers.

The presented above synergy effects from tourism business transnationalization, with all their parallel impacts on the process of tourist services' production, are gradually relocating corporations on a radically new level of management. At the same time, corporation product also gets new features which are necessary for the achievement of global competitive advantages. All of the latter are presented in this book with the prefix "hyper-" which assumes, first of all, the global scale of these competitive advantages, that is, company's capacity to use them at any regional or world tourism market. Secondly, this "hyper" nature of advantages means truly colossal opportunities the transnational companies obtain for all their further strategic and tactical activities. Thirdly, this means extremely low probability any of small or mid-sized tourism businesses at the same market would be able to reach similar competitive advantages and close enough level of competitiveness overall. The author suggests to consider all these hyper-advantages in the frameworks of the 6H model.

To these 6Hs mentioned above belong: hyper-profit, hyper-competitiveness, hyper-presence, hyper-positioning, hyper-mobility and finally, hyper-prospects.

In our observations, today many TNCs in tourism tend to apply these hyper-advantages in relation to national states and the tourism sector as such.

Transnational corporations operating in tourism guarantee their home countries not only large-scale implementation of rather "selfish" model of outbound tourism (economically convenient for this home country) but also full protection of the internal tourism market from penetration of foreign representatives operating in the same sector.

Expansion of corporations at foreign tourist market indeed initially "washes out" significant funds from the economies of their home countries, however, it also promotes outbound tourism. It stimulates capital outflow from a country - but at the same time it also increases, and significantly, the financial indicators of corporate performance. Expanding geographically, TNC enlarges not the circle of its suppliers and partners abroad (though this too) but rather the assortment of their tourist offers. Therefore, the home countries of corporations are usually well aware of TNCs' vital role for their economies. Thus, they are strongly motivated to encourage corporate expansion of large tourist business, supplying with all instruments they can, including those of political pressure.

Relations of transnational corporations with recipient countries are not that obvious, on the opposite, they are often contradictory. In this regard we need to mention that the capital invested by corporations in the economies of recipient countries still remains integral part of corporate reproduction process.

Integrating labor force from various countries worldwide and setting nearly the same requirements to all their staff worldwide, TNCs play a vital role in popularization of international standards in HR preparation. This, in its turn, leads to qualitative growth of tourism production in the recipient countries, and consequently, also to the growth of labor productivity. TNCs are also strong enough to impose their influence on local authorities, thus changing taxation regimes, simplifying bureaucratic procedures, encouraging the provision of better conditions for investments and privatization.

However, there is also a range of problems in relations of TNCs with recipient economies. This concerns, first of all, the activities that contradict the interests of the latter. These problems, inter alia, include: using corporate power to impose too much of pressure of local, much smaller, tourist firms; setting monopolistic prices; tax evasive behavior (most frequently using transfer pricing and other schemes to direct funds from one country to another); predatory exploitation of local tourist potential and resources; causing environmental problems; contributing to brain drain (from a recipient country to the country of corporations' headquarters); political lobbying on the issues which would be economically disadvantageous for the recipient economy. The latter of the mentioned problems might be the most risky for the recipient economies, since such corporate lobbying limits significantly both political and economic independence of national states in their relations with TNCs and in general. On the other hand, this is yet another proof for TNCs' features of hyper-positioning.

Hyper-advantages of transnational corporations also impact the tourism sector itself, on the global scale. The aim of any tourist TNC is to have the maximum possible share of future profits using the maximum of all arising opportunities. And any company with such an ambitious aim would have to increase its influence to the level of overall sectoral influence. Already today large tourism business is able regulate the world tourism market, and this business regulation is much more efficient than the regulation practiced by politicians and national governments.

The fifth chapter of this book considers in great details the process and problems of the organizational structure formation by TNCs. Their organizational structure must be oriented, first of all, on permanent management imposed by a parent company in relation to its foreign branches. At the same time, managers in these foreign branches should have enough freedom for independent decision-making, especially when it comes to the issues of consumer demand satisfaction, taking into account the specific features of local markets and the peculiarities of national legislation.

Traditional approaches to organizational structures of companies that are still used by managers and that are based on linear, functional and linear-functional models, are of little use for TNCs due to the fact that classical models always assume strict structuring and rather static forms of organization, both being impossible in the transnational corporate environment.

Within the frameworks of contemporary tourist TNC strict and stable structuring would be hardly possible. Moreover, principles and priorities of corporate structuring are changing all the time, reacting dynamically to both internal changes and external factors.

Retrospective analysis of TNCs' activities in the tourism sector allows us outlining several central approaches to organizational structuring based on divisional management and creation of various sorts of alliances and other unions (including strategic business zones - SBZ, and centers of investments inside corporations). Both these mentioned above models used to be quite popular among transnational companies in the near past. However, several drawbacks in such structuring along with the growing necessity to take tourism specificity into account lead us to the need to determine new principles of the organizational structures' formation, those related to the so-called adaptive models.

Adaptive structures have the following key features: absence or minor influence of bureaucratic regulation; no exact division between the types of labor; blurred borders between the levels of management and their low number in general; maximum flexibility of the management structure; decentralized decision-making; individual responsibility of each employee for overall performance. Besides that, adaptive organizational structure has the following capacities:

- changing its form and shape so that to adapt to the quickly changing environment;

- speeding up the implementation of the most complex projects and programmes;

- limited timespan only, that is, such structures are being used only per particular problem solving, for a certain project or program;

- introduction of interim management bodies, also with a limited timespan.

Within tourist TNCs middle levels of management have experienced the most significant transformations. This can be also explained by high dynamics of changes in the external environment of international tourism. Constantly changing market environment means companies are forced to reorient all activities of their structural units and those of their SBZs on much narrower segments of consumers since competition at the tourism market these days is happening on a rather individualized level.

Chapter 5 of this monograph offers the author's own X model of organizational structure for a contemporary tourist TNC. This model fits the today's context because it captures well the network nature of corporations operating in the tourism sector today. The offered here X model is based on the principles of adaptive structuring of management with its emphasis on the middle level (cooperation in teams; more meaningful role of highly qualified professionals in management, even those who do not have enough skills and knowledge for operational or strategic management; active use of project management; maximum orientation of business processes on the client; autonomous work of teams; low level of bureaucracy; flexible hierarchy etc). At the same time, the model distinguishes between three core types of activities inside corporations (creative, managerial and operational) and also between the fields within which these types of activities are carried out (virtual, intangible, tangible and technological).

According to the suggested model, any corporation operating today in the tourism sector can be understood as an open network, in which terminal units are presented by various divisions and strategic business zones. Exact location of these divisions and zones cannot be regulated or even specified exactly (as it used to be in the hierarchical organizational structures) due to the fact that their relations between each other and with the central authority (the Board, first of all) is determined not by their location but rather by the contents, role and orientation of the value chains introduced and implemented by corporate top management.

Dynamic nature of organizational interactions inside a corporation is predetermined by the necessity to boost flexibility under the constantly changing conditions at the tourism market. Another contributing factor is the multitude of divisions, departments and groups within the network structure of a corporation, many of them carrying out similar or nearly similar types of operations.

The latter goes against the traditional principle of labor distribution and does not allow forming stable production relations within the corporate framework. For example, one and the same TNC may own several airlines, several hotel chains and also agent networks. Units inside these groups are performing exactly the same functions, thus, they happen to be in competition with each other.

When a corporate Board is developing a certain promising project (thus creating also a new value chain), it may engage as many components from the network as it wishes, and these components may be similar in functions sometimes. The key criteria for inclusion is how current performance indicators of a certain structural unit match the requirements posed to the potential participants of this project.

Presence of subdivisions and terminal units with very much similar production functions means they are able to serve as substitutions for each other, and this, in turn, is yet another manifestation of company's flexibility and adaptiveness. Under such circumstances the Board always has alternatives to consider for its larger projects of strategic importance. Also, this situation provides the Board with plentiful opportunities for further optimization of production activities.

Unity of such a transnational tourism network is successfully maintained due to the following:

- each structural group or strategic business zone has its top manager, and together these top managers form some sort of "human skeleton" of a TNC;

- there is quite a strict code of conduct along with the system of the related ethical and professional rules (all equally applicable to top managers, creative professionals and operational-level managers). All these rules not only regulate the behavior of all employees, but also propagate corporate values and priorities;

- the Board is being permanently engaged in the development and implementation of corporate projects, introducing new value chains, including and excluding certain structural units into/from these projects and value chains;

- there is always a set of instruments to increase/decrease the entry/exit barriers for any of the participants within the corporate network;

- vast majority of all interactions, both external and intracorporate, are transparent.

Therefore, the network structure of a TNC has the following key features: the minimal number of levels in management; dynamic nature of internal interactions; total absence of overregulated horizontal connections; communication based on strategic partnership and other forms of deals inside the network; no labor distribution principles inside the corporation; network serving as a skeleton in which key units are represented by top managers and/or strategic business zones; openness of corporate environment to the external world.

Transnational companies operating in the tourism sector are also able to apply the same network approach outside their corporate structure, in their relations with various external factors. For example, they may use networking while establishing relations with independent intermediaries, active consumers of their tourist product or even with state authorities.

Significant differences in organization of tourism production, normative and legal infrastructure for corporate management, development of financial institutions have predetermined the parallel existence of various corporate types in the tourism sector. Some of these specific types have been considered in the final chapter of this monograph.

First, the author describes the American model of tourist corporation, specificity of which concerns the determining roles of financial markets and minor shareholders. Other important features of the American model include: direct correlation between top manager's success and securities' prices; orientation on mergers and acquisitions, especially when it concerns the objects with significant material & technical basis.

Then the key features of the European (German) tourist corporations have been outlined: prominent role of the banking sector; less dependence from the situation at the stock markets - and consequently, more attention being paid to the strategic priorities of the company itself, which is especially relevant at the initial stages, requiring serious spending and also often overcoming the resistance of influential shareholders. These key features of the German model which has been dominating at the European market for quite a while were rooting in the individualization of tourist services in general. And all of the above allowed European tourist corporations, already back in the 1980s, close the deals in which the core objects were intangible assets. At that time, the same was literally impossible for tourist corporations of the American type.

Islamic tourist corporations were gradually emerging and developing under the conditions of rather limited access to bank assets. Another limitation was the ban on interest rates and interest payments, and also on some other, related, financial operations. Even though this was a serious limiting factor at the beginning - all the related limitations provoked the emergence of rather original, unusual for the West, forms of cooperation between tourism companies with each other, and also with the banks. All these relations were based not on distribution of results from all related economic activities but rather on mutual responsibility of partners for the implementation of projects. In this context mutual responsibility provides additional opportunities and even the whole brand new platform for further transnationalization.

Bibliography

Andreeva E., Ushakov, D. (2016). Internal regional and demographic tourists' inflows distribution as factor of national tourism competitiveness. *Actual Problem of Economics*, 9.

Bakan, J. (2004). *The Corporation: The Pathological Pursuit of Profit and Power*. New York: Free.

Bandurin A. (1999). *Corporative activity*. Moscow, Bukvitsa. (in Russian)

Borrus M., Zusman J. (1997). *Wintelism and the changing terms of global competition: prototype of the future*. BRIE Working paper, Berkeley.

Bradley M., Desai A., Kim E. (1988). Synergetic gains from corporate acquisitions and their division between the stockholders of target and acquiring firms. *Journal of Financial Economics*, 21.

Crotty, E. (1998). *Multinational corps in neo-liberal regime*. Cambridge University Press.

Drucker, P. (1966). *The Effective Executive. The Definitive Guide to Getting the Right Things Done*. Harper Business

Goldsmith, R., Flynn, R. (1992). Identifying Innovators in Consumer Product Markets. *European Journal of Marketing*, 26,12.

Gulyaev, V. (2003). *Tourism: economy and social development*. Moscow. Finansy i statistika. (in Russian)

Holstein, W. (1990). The Stateless Corporation. *Business Week* .

Howe, S. (2002). *Empire: A Very Short Introduction*. Oxford: Oxford UP.

Jeffrey, A. & Painter, J. (2009). *Imperialism and Post colonialism. Political Geography: An Introduction to Space and Power*. London: SAGE, 174-75.

Khairiree, M. D., Ushakov, D. (2016). Sufficiency Economy as an Alter-Globalist Development Concept: Topicality Factors and Conditions Needed For Introduction. *The EUrASEANs*, 1.

Kirillov A., Vinichenko M., Makuchkin S., Melnichuk A., Ushakov, D. (2017). Career Opportunities for the Management's Personnel Reserve. Eurasian J Anal Chem; 12.

Konina N. (2005). *M&A in competitiveness of international companies*. Moscow, Prospect. (in Russian)

Lenskiy E. (2001). *Transnationalizations of capital*. Minsk, Armita – marketing and management. (in Russian)

Marrying in haste (2000). *Financial Times*, 12.04.

Micklethwait, J., Wooldridge, A. (2003). *The company: A short history of a revolutionary idea*. New York: Modern Library.

Mikhailushkin, A., Shimko, P. (2005). *Economy of transnational company*. Moscow, High School. (in Russian).

Movsesyan, A. (2001). *Transnationalization in the world economy*. Moscow. Financial Academy under the Russia Government. (in Russian).

Pinto A., Vincentini G. (1998). *The legal basis of Corporate Governance in Publicly Held Corporations*. Kluver Law International.

Robins, N. (2006). *This Imperious Company. The Corporation That Changed the World How the East India Company Shaped the Modern Multinational*. London: Pluto.

Roy, D., Seim, V. , Coppett, J. (1992). Global Logistics and Stateless Corporations. *Transportation Practitioners Journal*. 59, 2.

Rudykh, N. (2000). Market of corporative control in the Russian Federation. *Finansist*, 11. (in Russian)

Rudykh, N. (2005). *Conglomerate M&A*. Moscow, Delo. (in Russian)

Savchuk S. (2002). Analyze of basic motives of merges and acquisitions. *Management in Russia and abroad.* 5. (in Russian)

Sivash, O.S., Burkaltseva, D.D., Ushakov, D.S. (2017). Activization of investment process in the agrarian sector. *International Journal of Ecology and Development*, 38/4.

Transnational Corporations in World Development (1988). United Nations.

Tretyakov M. (2004). Convergence of corporate governance models. *Issues of economy*, 1. (in Russian)

Ushakov D. (2006). *National Tourism Industry: problems of development*. Moscow, Granitsa. (in Russian)

Ushakov D. (2017c). Information Technologies Within Market Economy: How Communication Tools Became A Field Of Activity. *The EUrASEANs*, 1.

Ushakov, D. (2016). Dynamics of international economical relationships in the global context of innovative modernization. *International Journal of Environmental and Science Education*, 18.

Ushakov, D., Bandurin, V., Bandurin, A. (2017b). Taxation regime as a factor of mutually integrated macroeconomic systems' dynamics. *Montenegrin Journal of Economics*, 13.

Ushakov, D., Elokhova, I., Kozonogova, E. (2017a). Post industrialization prospects in the dynamics of socioeconomic transformations: Cluster approach. *International Journal of Ecological Economics and Statistics*, 38/2.

Ushakov, D., Kharchenko, L. (2017). Environmental factors of national competitiveness in modern MNCs' development. *International Journal of Ecological Economics and Statistics*, 38/2.

Ushakov, D., Simasathiansophon, N. (2016). Transnationalization as a trend of the present stage of international tourism development. *Actual Problems of Economics*, 2

Van, H.T., Huu, A.T., Ushakov, D.(2017). Liberal reforms & economic growth: Current issues and interrelations. *Journal of International Studies*.

Voorhees, R., Seim, E., Coppett, J. (1992). Global Logistics and Stateless Corporations. *Transportation Practitioners Journal*. 59, 2.

Wilkins, M. (1992). *The Growth of Multinationals*. Harper Business.

World Investment Report 2016: Cross-border mergers and acquisitions and development. (2017). New York and Geneva: UNCTAD.

Zdorov A. (2003). *Economy of tourism*. Moscow. Finansy i statistika (in Russian).

Zhdanov, N. (2003). *Islamic model of the world order*. Moscow, International relationships. (in Russian)

Zhuravlyov, A. (2000). Islam and economics. *Russia and Muslim world*. 4 (94). (in Russian)

Zuglevich V. (2003). *Corporative management in the conditions of market non-stability*. Moscow. Examen. (in Russian)

www.ingramcontent.com/pod-product-compliance
Lightning Source LLC
Chambersburg PA
CBHW071426180526
45170CB00001B/237